CREATURES ON THE EDGE

Wildlife Along the Lower Rio Grande

CREATURES ON THE EDGE

Wildlife Along the Lower Rio Grande

THE VALLEY LAND FUND WILDLIFE PHOTO CONTEST II

CHACHALACA PRESS

MCALLEN, TEXAS

Cover: *Wendy Shattil & Bob Rozinski / Cook Ranches - Jim & Kathy Collins*
Back Cover: *Michael H. Francis / McAllen Properties - James A. McAllen; Glenn Hayes & Bill Draker / Dr. Gary M. Schwarz;*
Mike Kelly / Garcia Ranch - J. A. Garcia; Irene Sacilotto / H. Yturria Land & Cattle Co.

First Printing, 1997
Text & Photography Copyright © 1997 by The Valley Land Fund

ISBN 0-9660013-0-3

Published for The Valley Land Fund by

Chachalaca Press
2701 N. 30th, Suite 2
McAllen, Texas 78501

Editors / Jan Epton Seale, Dr. Steve Bentsen, Colleen Curran Hook
Printing coordination and color work / Bob Carter
Book and cover design / Erren Seale

The Valley Land Fund
P. O. Box 2891
McAllen, Texas 78502

(956) 381-1264   FAX (956) 381-1794

Grateful acknowledgment is made to Pantheon Books, a division of Random House, Inc. for permission to quote David Abram from *The Spell of the Sensuous* (Pantheon Books, New York, 1996). Copyright © 1996 by David Abram.
Printed in Canada

Dedicated to the memory of

JOHN THOMAS ROBERTSON

who embraced the natural world with open arms and loving spirit.
May John's wisdom, counsel, concern, resiliency, and sense of adventure
inspire other young people of the Valley to love and care for the land.

January 11, 1975 — March 12, 1994

C O N T E N T S

THE WINNING PHOTOGRAPHS

This book was created to alter your breathing—
to cause you to gasp in astonishment;
to aspirate an appreciative "ahhh";
to form words clearly in advocacy for its subject;
and
to whisper its knowledge to your children and their children.

The animal universe has always been with us. The power of the camera lens to disclose that universe brings to us both unique blessing and awesome responsibility.

We sit comfortably turning the beautiful pages, away from the testiness of the javelina and the rattlesnake. We do not have to climb to the eagle's aerie or burrow to the mouse's lair. The animals stay still for us, their eyes shining, their bodies taut with action or slack in repose, their skin, hair, or feathers luminous in the genius of the photographer's skills. With images somehow eternally alert and sentient, and thus transcending reality for the moment, they cause us to enter a magical perfect world.

We claim our right to be filled with joy, to be awestruck, to be transported by the variety, complexity, handsomeness, fierceness, even cosmic humor inherent in these beasts.

But somewhere in the deep brush graze their living counterparts. Overhead soars the real nighthawk. Wading across a stream is the virtual armadillo. And in our own backyards the dragonfly, the monarch, the hummer stir the air. With the knowledge of their reality comes choice.

When we pause to marvel at the book-bound critters, we must forever be changed by the realization that, miraculous as the art of photography is, each image only bespeaks the essence of the real creatures *out there.*

And, like a mythic first family, no longer ignorant of the animals' existence, we begin to ask the hard questions. What is our place in relation to them? What about our encroachment on their worlds?

How can we diverse beings live side by side, given the ever-growing demands that our complex world places on finite natural resources? How important are wild animals to our society and are we willing to hold a portion of our world sacred for them?

We human inhabitants of the Lower Rio Grande Valley of Texas ask these questions of our wildlife for more urgent reasons. Here at the end of the twentieth century, we live in this southernmost triangle of Texas and the U.S.A., sobered by the explosive growth from phenomenal human migrations and sweeping international economic and political change. All this, and the lingering nostalgic penchant for individual freedom—the right to do whatever one wants to with one's property —that has traditionally characterized an American frontier.

The joy is free. Turn the pages of this book and be moved by the wildness and diversity therein. Respond to the exotic and common, the abundant and rare, the fierce and the timid.

Let your praise go to the caring landowners— whether ranchers, farmers, suburb- or city-dwellers— under whose grace the animals are allowed to live. Express your appreciation to those many individual, group, and corporate sponsors who made the Wildlife Photo Contest a reality by their generous underwriting.

It will, of course, be easy to appreciate the photographers who did the hard, patient field work of bringing these images to you in your easy chair. And, if you're so inclined, thank a Divine Consciousness who thought up the blessed creatures of the earth.

But the knowledge is not free. Astounding as the thought is, in a world like ours, the everlastingness of many of these animals is a grave doubt.

So let the pleasure you receive from this beautiful book be translated to attitudes: caring, respect for non-humankind, sharing; and to action: study, educating the young, conserving and preserving resources, sounding alarms when they are threatened.

Paradoxically, caring about animals, for what is not human, brings out one of the better traits in the human animal. Let us work for a world shared with other creatures, for such a world will always be infinitely more pleasurable and sacred to both us and them.

We did not put the animals here. We do not own them. But we are responsible, in our overcrowded, overused world, for their existence and well-being. We are indeed our animal-brothers' keepers.

Jan Epton Seale

McAllen, Texas 1997

THE EDGE: THE LOWER RIO GRANDE VALLEY OF TEXAS

As you turn the pages of this book, taking the wildlife tour of the Lower Rio Grande Valley, you will no doubt be impressed by the diversity of animals in the area, as well as the settings in which they crawl, graze, stalk, jump, run, swim, flit and fly.

You have a right to amazement. The Lower Rio Grande Valley of Texas—bounded on the east by the Gulf of Mexico, on the south by the Rio Grande River, on the west by Cambrian limestone hills, and on the north by a vast savannah—is a unique region in the Western Hemisphere.

The Valley (a puzzling moniker to first-time visitors) is the extreme tip of a huge area south of San Antonio known simply as South Texas. Photographs of the animals featured in these pages were taken in four counties: Cameron, Willacy, Hidalgo, and Starr.

In this area approximately 160 miles east to west along the Rio Grande River, and about 60 miles north to south, we find seashore, palm grove, river woodland, grassland, and brush country. Geologically, the Lower Rio Grande Valley is an alluvial plain, a very broad delta where the 1,800-mile Rio Grande River flows into the Gulf of Mexico.

A blend of peoples, language, and customs between the Americas, this area is also a biological melting pot resulting from its position between North and South America. Vast migrations of birds occur overland and on nearby waterways as flyways converge, while many resident species of animals exist here on the northern or southern limits of their defined ranges.

The landscape of the Valley has experienced two cataclysmic changes in the last century. Around 1900, entrepreneurs, realizing the economic potential of the rich soil, began to clear the vast tangle of lush vegetation for the purpose of agricultural development. Citrus orchards and cotton fields replaced brush, range, and thickets.

Today, from those cleared lands, the Valley's citrus and vegetable crops are recognized and appreciated worldwide. A 341-day growing season and irrigation from the Rio Grande allow intensive farming of these and of cotton, sorghum, and sugarcane, as well as of other newly introduced crops.

Now, a century hence, change again is taking place. A mild climate, close proximity to Mexico, friendly people and a buyer's economy beckon thousands of retired folk from the North each year. Add to this a significant number of vacationing Mexican nationals and North Americans and a sizeable influx of Central American immigrants seeking economic betterment.

But here at the close of the century, these gradual and somewhat accommodated phenomena pale beside a larger event. With the signing of the North American Free Trade Agreement in 1992, attention to the Lower Rio Grande Valley as a trade route has caused sudden, huge growth in almost every area of life.

Import/export businesses, trucking, international banking and law, border passage enforcement, and the maquiladora "twin plant" industry have required vast complexes. In turn, the swell in population brought on by these new entities has mandated vast new housing, schools, medical facilities, shopping centers, and professional buildings.

The Valley will never be the sleepy little province some claim it once was, deplored for its geographic isolation and lack of facilities to accommodate modern tastes. We must believe that our sudden expansion will in many ways upgrade the quality of life here.

On the other hand, such unprepared-for growth has brought with it a multitude of problems. Many of these, particularly the need for housing, public services, and new roadways, are being addressed in an expeditious, even emergency-like manner.

But a moment of contemplation brings a question of greatest gravity. What happens to the *land* in such a place? Our most ambitious political and economic achievements are worthless if the earth space we inhabit cannot, in the end, accommodate the rich animal and plant life for which it was intended.

Whatever we may become economically, politically, and culturally, we are, to begin with, beings subject to the laws of the natural world. We are cohabitants of the Valley with all the other animals. We are part of the ecosystem. We are wildlife too.

So are our children and their children after. Political and economic conditions will wax and wane but the land, with its supporting flora and fauna, should be our first concern. Not all the wealth in the world, with its attendant pleasures of technological know-how and luxuriant privilege, can supplant our need as humans to see trees, hear bird calls, recognize an animal's footprint in the mud.

The Valley is not Anywhere, U.S.A. This delicate, picturesque terrain, with its convergence of unusual plant and animal life, is the first concern of the Valley Land Fund.

Just now, when you are pausing to let these images of our Valley animals enter your consciousness, thrilling you with their mystery and beauty, remember that their future existence is no longer a certainty.

They will have a place here tomorrow only by our highest intentions and noblest endeavors. We must look beyond the easy dollars, the lure of "progress," a philosophy that asks us, astonishingly, to consider even the natural world hopelessly outdated.

We cannot afford the loneliness and ugliness of a Valley devoid of animals. Preserving a home for them is not optional.

WHAT IS THE VALLEY LAND FUND?

In the course of the twentieth century, about ninety-five percent of the natural habitat in the Valley, home for centuries of special plants and animals, has been lost by expansion of agriculture, commerce, and human population.

The Valley Land Fund was organized in l987 by a small group of Valley residents concerned about this loss. Their goal is to preserve the remaining three- to five-percent of native wildlife habitat, to expand that percentage if possible, and to enhance these lands through a variety of means.

Broadened in l997 to a 40-member board, The Valley Land Fund sponsors educational programs, holds special events, gathers information about current natural growth holdings, encourages conservation, and defines economic incentives for interested land-holders.

The major fundraiser and educational tool for The Valley Land Fund is its Wildlife Photo Contest. The brainchild of John and Audrey Martin, the first contest, held in l994, offered $77,250 in awards and attracted eighty-eight photographers teaming up with fifty-one Valley landowners. The overall success of that first contest culminated in great popularity of the first book of photos, from a public hungry for a closer interpretive look at the fascinating creatures around them.

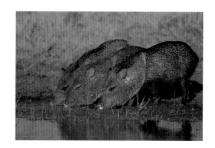

THE VALLEY LAND FUND WILDLIFE PHOTO CONTEST II

It is a hot summer day in 1996.
On the third floor of McAllen Memorial Library,
volunteers from The Valley Land Fund move dream-
like between long tables laden with huge albums.
They are carefully labeling and sorting over 5,000
slides of animal photos entered in the second Valley
Land Fund Wildlife Photo Contest.

Among the group—fluctuating in personnel all day
as schedules permit—are the specialists:
field biologists, scientists, ardent birders; and other
more generalized folk: teachers, accountants,
secretaries, retirees, parents—who bring their love of
feather, fur, and claw and a gift of their time
to help in this monumental endeavor . . . .

Capitalizing on the great success of the first wildlife photo contest in 1994, The Valley Land Fund in 1996 again sponsored a competition. The mission of the project was threefold: 1) to highlight the Lower Rio Grande Valley's unique animals and their threatened habitat; 2) to create an incentive for landowners to protect wildlife habitat; and 3) to capture the images of the diverse wildlife for use in education and promotion of the area.

The 1996 tournament of cameras attracted photographers the world over and resulted in a collection of 185 prize-winning photographs, judged by three nationally known authorities in wildlife photography: David Baxter, the editor of *Texas Parks and Wildlife*; John Nuhn, photo editor of *National Wildlife* and *International Wildlife,* publications of the National Wildlife Federation; and Thomas A. Wiewandt, Ph.D., nature photographer and owner of a photographic safari business.

Partnered with the photographers were 108 landowners, who welcomed photographers to some 250,000 acres of private property in four counties: Cameron, Willacy, Hidalgo, and Starr. Prize money of $100,000 was shared equally between these landowners and their visiting photographers.

Dedicated businesses and individual sponsors who underwrote the competition with their generous donations made the contest possible. The Valley Land Fund is forever in their debt for stepping forward to support this project. A complete listing of sponsors, along with photographers, landowners, judges, and prizewinners may be found following the photographs.

The contest consisted of five divisions: Birds, Mammals, Insects & Arachnids, Reptiles & Amphibians, and a division called "Scenics with Wildlife" in which the landscapes surrounding the animals were emphasized. A special competition featured small-tract and backyard wildlife. These groupings were subdivided into 52 classes of species or groups of wildlife.

In compliance with the rules of the contest, all photographs were taken in a six-month period between January and June of 1996. And they were all taken on the designated contest-entered properties located in Cameron, Willacy, Hidalgo, and Starr counties.

The book of the 1994 contest, **Treasures of South Texas,** sold out quickly. This second book, **Creatures on the Edge: Wildlife Along the Lower Rio Grande,** is expanded to reflect the growth of the contest and heightened interest in ecology and habitat in the Valley. In these pages the thoughts of prize-winning landowners and photographers are explored.

Introductions to each of the sections highlight Valley birds, mammals, insects and arachnids, and reptiles and amphibians. We've also included a number of honorable mentions so worthy they begged to be shared along with the top prizewinners. And you'll find the winning photos of the highly popular Fourth Grade Nature Photo Contest.

The Valley Land Fund hopes that this unique contest and the resulting book will serve as a prototype for similar competitions sponsored by other groups worldwide, all drawing attention to the great need to save our planet's wildlife.

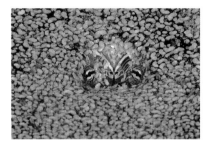

. . . Now the group in the library has been bent over the tables for six hours. Some have gone briefly to the corner to eat a carry-in taco or call home that they'll be a little longer. Eyes strain; backs ache; feet grow heavy. The human volunteer of the Valley Land Fund is beginning to show a little stress.

Then someone at the far end of the table lets out a great sigh. "Wow! Come and look at this!"

Everyone stops, mentally putting a comma on the task at hand, and gathers around.

There's a green parakeet with a gleaming drop of water suspended from its beak, or a black-tailed jackrabbit, ears glowing coral in afternoon sun. Maybe it's a den of bobcat kittens, their eyes polished with new existence, or a velvet-antlered deer nuzzling its reflected image as it slakes its thirst at the edge of a pond.

For a moment, the two-legged catalogers are as still as the animals paused on the slides they peer at. They have their own timeless moment, each wrapped in a private world of analysis, discovery, awe, or alleluia.

It's the best kind of work break.

Back to work, everybody! Only 3,247 slides to go.

THE GRAND PRIZE PHOTOGRAPHERS

We asked our photographers who won Grand Prizes in the contest to put down their cameras for a moment and become storytellers. Did they have a memorable moment during their work in The Valley Land Fund Wildlife Photo Contest? Here are some of their replies:

"Of the entire six months of the contest, there is one afternoon that stands out in our minds. One of us had been in our photo blind next to a pond for about four hours on a hot and windy day when a five-foot-long diamond-back rattlesnake came from behind the blind and glided past. Twenty inches further south and the snake would have come through the back of the blind. It went to the edge of the pond, coiled, and drank. It was so intent that it didn't interrupt its drinking while we walked to the edge of the pond to photograph it."

Wendy Shattil & Bob Rozinski -
Denver, Colorado
Cook Ranches
FIRST GRAND PRIZE

"One of my first goals was to photograph Least Grebes with young. After setting up a blind near a nest in January, I spent time in that blind each month waiting for young. Unfortunately, between flooding and/or predators, I never had any luck. Finally, in June, on my last day in Texas, I went to the blind and would you believe it?!—the adults had six youngsters swimming around them!"

Michael H. Francis - Billings, Montana
McAllen Properties
SECOND GRAND PRIZE

"My favorite wildlife encounter was with a beautiful bobcat that came bounding up to within ten feet of me the first time I called her in. I had hoped my new predator call device would work, but the bobcat's fearless, open demeanor took me by complete surprise."

Mike Kelly - Terrell, Texas
J.A. Garcia Ranch
THIRD GRAND PRIZE

"Early in the contest I had been trying, unsuccessfully, for several mornings to get some shots of deer in the first light of morning. Low clouds in the east always seemed to get in the way. Then one morning, there were no clouds and the light was perfect on the spot where I had placed some corn to lure the deer. But still no deer. I looked down for a moment and was thinking about what I would give to have a deer in that light.

When I looked back up, there he was. He only stayed a moment, but I was able to shoot about a dozen frames and I placed 2nd in the deer category with one of the shots."

Glenn Hayes - Markham, Texas
El Tecomate Ranch—Dr. Gary Schwarz
FOURTH GRAND PRIZE

"My partner and I were trying to photograph skunks and he got too close. I had to live with that smell for a whole week!"

Bill Draker - San Antonio, Texas
El Tecomate Ranch—Dr. Gary Schwarz
FOURTH GRAND PRIZE

"From the first day I saw the Yturria, I fell in love with the ranch. One afternoon from one of my blinds situated near a pond, I counted at least fifteen different species of birds within my field of view and photo range. They varied from Black-bellied Whistling-Ducks & Spotted Sandpipers to Black Terns & White-faced Ibis just a few feet away."

Irene Hinke-Sacilotto - Joppa, Maryland
H. Yturria Land & Cattle Co.
FIFTH GRAND PRIZE

"Gracious hospitality is a hallmark of your region. I was invited, one afternoon, to an informal dinner party at one of the properties where I was photographing. We ate outside on picnic tables. As the evening was progressing, a Walking Stick appeared on the bench next to us. Rather than sit on it, we moved it to a nearby branch where it stayed. Later, I got my camera gear back out and photographed it."

James Allen Murray - Arlington, Texas
Marsha and Mike Gamel Property
FIRST GRAND PRIZE / SMALL TRACT &
BACKYARD COMPETITION

"During the 1996 Valley Land Fund Contest, I was patiently waiting for an uncooperative Buff-bellied Hummingbird to land on that certain twig when I heard something scratching around on the top of my portable blind. All of a sudden one of those perpetually perturbed South Texas fussbudgets, the Bewick's Wren, popped into the blind, gave me an irate glare, scolded me thoroughly, and then satisfied, popped back out."

Hugh Lieck - Kingsville, Texas
David & Diane Garza Property
THIRD GRAND PRIZE / SMALL TRACT &
BACKYARD COMPETITION

...FURTHER THOUGHTS

We also asked them why they decided to enter the contest. All were honest enough to say up-front that the $100,000 in prize money was a big incentive. But they also found other reasons. Some had never been to the Valley and the promotional material whetted their sense of adventure.

The possibility of access to private ranches was another enticement. Irene Hinke-Sacilotto said, "By working on a private ranch, I was afforded privacy that I would not find on public lands so that I could focus on my photography with little disturbance."

And they all felt that the motive for the contest—calling attention to the need to save habitat for wildlife in a special place—was a worthy one, something that they wanted to be part of.

What was unique about photographing wildlife in South Texas?

"The many different species of critters," Bill Draker replied. "You never knew what you were going to see next." Jim Murray felt that "the area ranks right up there with the Florida Everglades, Bosque Del Apache and Yellowstone National Park. It is now on my short list of favorite wildlife areas for viewing and photography!"

Of course, some were candid enough to mention the "hazards of reptiles, bugs, cactus and thorns" and the "very hot and windy" days they experienced. One commented that "the only place we've found to be more difficult to photograph than South Texas is the tropical rain forest."

Still, our hospitality received a 100% "yea" vote. It is a great compliment to all our sponsors and landowners that the photographers noted in their South Texas visits "incredibly gracious hospitality and generosity of all we met."

What would they, with the sharp eyes of visitors and photographers, tell us who make our homes here? "I would urge local residents to view their homes from the air. So little of 'wild' Texas is left for the wildlife," commented Michael H. Francis.

"I was very impressed by the people and the region. The unique efforts of The Valley Land Fund to both preserve and showcase the wildlife of the area are to be highly commended," wrote Jim Murray.

"Wild things bring a measure of balance and sanity to our chaotic world, giving us hope and inspiration to preserve what remains," Wendy Shattil and Bob Rozinski observed.

"South Texas has an unbelievable variety of wildlife," Glenn Hayes said. "If we can save the habitat, we can save the wildlife."

OTHER GRAND PRIZE WINNERS

Charles Melton - Boulder, Colorado
John & Audrey Martin
BEST OF CONTEST - JUDGES' VOTE

Mary Jo Janovsky & Michelle Moss - Harlingen, Texas
Rio Grande Valley Shooting Center
BEST OF CONTEST - POPULAR VOTE

Charles Melton - Boulder, Colorado
John & Audrey Martin
SECOND GRAND PRIZE (TIE) / SMALL TRACT & BACKYARD COMPETITION

Lance Krueger - McAllen, Texas
Rita K. Roney
SECOND GRAND PRIZE (TIE) / SMALL TRACT & BACKYARD COMPETITION

THE GRAND PRIZE LANDOWNERS

"I wonder if the ground has anything to say. I wonder if the ground is listening to what is said," spoke Young Chief of the Cayuses tribe in 1855.

The ground in the Lower Rio Grande Valley indeed has much to say. And the ground is also listening. Attention to the voice and spirit of the land is strong in landowners who entered their land in The Valley Land Fund Wildlife Photo Contest.

Many landowners can appreciate the deep feelings for and tender care of the land by their forebears. James McAllen, of McAllen Properties, comments, "Since 1932, A.A. McAllen has created a wildlife refuge within his domain and taught his heirs the appreciation of their environs." Jim Collins, of Cook Ranches, observes of his late father-in-law, "Vannie Cook was first a lover of wildlife, nature, and the outdoors. Everything else had to be in balance with those passions."

Danny Butler, manager of the H. Yturria Land & Cattle Co., speaks of the spirit of caring for the land of his great-great grandfather, Francisco Yturria, who bought the ranch in 1858. "I think he would expect me to do nothing less than what we are doing for it today."

For others, their inheritance is one of spirit more than blood ties. Owners of the Garcia Ranch, Sue Ann and J.A. Garcia, Jr., comment that some of the previous owners of their ranch "were very caring to the balance of nature," believing that "the land and wildlife God put here was to provide them with food and shelter."

El Tecomate Ranch, uniquely owned by seven land conservationists, was purchased from the V.H. Guerra family, who had owned it for several generations. Virgil Guerra Sr. had a special love for the brush and wildlife of the San Roman Ranch at a time when land-clearing and increasing domestic production were in vogue. After his death, his widow and children carried on his ideals for the care of the land and wildlife. Gary Schwarz, one of the present owners of El Tecomate, describes the current feeling toward Mr. Guerra's lasting influence. "Our portion of San Roman, the Tecomate pasture, honors his memory and the two ranches continue to be managed as one and as he would have wished."

Some Valley landowners, however, must create their land's heritage. Twelve years ago, when John and Audrey Martin purchased their 30 acres in northern

SACLIOTTO / H. YTURRIA LAND & CATTLE CO.

Hidalgo County, it was a grain field. There were no trees or shrubs, and of course, very little wildlife. They lovingly hand-planted their acreage with native plants and now they describe it as "an ark," containing many representative Valley plants, with all the attendant wildlife that such plants attract.

Marsha and Mike Gamel's property near Mission consists of 17 acres of brush and a small lake, with a whimsical house built of native materials. Their property, which has never been cleared, is a sanctuary for birds in an area of the Valley which has shown intense appropriation of land recently for residential and business use.

• • • • •

When owners speak of these family-inherited or acquired lands, the key words are stewardship, commitment, and responsibility. They see the land as passing through their hands in the present, on loan from the past and with promises for the future.

James McAllen speaks of the landowner as "custodian" and "committed steward." Gary Schwarz places high priority on the role of stewardship, observing that the most unique thing about El Tecomate is the way seven dedicated people banded together in "a dream of owning and protecting the land and wildlife of South Texas."

In commitment is a mandate for determination and wisdom.

"The land is ours and it is our job, our obligation and commitment to hand it to the next generation in a condition that is conducive to the future and long-term preservation of all living things," affirms James McAllen.

Jim Collins urges flexible wisdom in land management: "Love and respect it and try to be flexible and change when needed."

Marsha and Mike Gamel observe wryly that we have to "take care of it" because "they're not building more of it!"

• • • • •

The large acreages along the Lower Rio Grande show an amazing diversity of plant and animal life.

For example, the J.A. Garcia Ranch lists among their wildlife: "white-tail deer, turkey, javelina, feral hogs, nilgai antelope, wild cats, armadillos, rabbits, raccoon, badgers, turtles, snakes and birds of all kinds."

The McAllen Properties have all native brush containing over 250 species of birds, 30 mammals, and 48 reptiles. "It's where the blue jay meets the green jay," James McAllen quips.

Landowners understand that wildlife management requires the utmost care and sensitivity. Jim Collins of Cook Ranches emphasizes the importance of research and study. He says, "We try to be flexible to meet changing conditions, and we try to balance habitat, wildlife, and our agribusiness concerns. We are constantly experimenting with feeding, genetics, and various large conservation techniques."

El Tecomate Ranch is an outstanding example of pro-active land and animal management. They cooperate with the Caesar Kleberg Wildlife Research Institute, plant extensive food plots for wildlife, and maintain feeding stations for deer and songbirds. Twenty miles of pipelines have been laid for wildlife watering stations, and photography blinds have been built.

Almost all landowners place voluntary restrictions on hunting wildlife on their properties. David and Diane Garza, owners of El Monte del Rancho Viejo in Cameron County, have left most of their land in thick, impenetrable brush. They have chosen not to allow hunting on their property for popular game birds such as doves and whitewing. James McAllen believes that "we should never harvest that which we cannot count and should nourish that which we can."

Gary Schwarz feels strongly the tie between responsible harvesting and preserving native South Texas habitat. "Even the songbirds and endangered plants benefit from habitat that is maintained for hunting," he observes.

Virtually all our contest landowners, whether their land is in cultivation or has been allowed to remain wild, stress the importance of supplying adequate food and water for their wildlife when it is not easily attainable by the animals from the land itself.

The H. Yturria Land & Cattle Co. has existed historically with a blend of cattle-raising and wildlife. The owners take care to preserve a balance on the land. Danny Butler, as manager of the ranch, reflected this attitude when he commented about the Wildlife Photo Contest, "We participated in it to show people of the Rio Grande Valley and South Texas that the ranchlands are much loved and are being well taken care of."

● ● ● ● ●

"Each new season brings something new," observe John and Audrey Martin of the land tract they call "our big backyard." Sue Ann and J.A. Garcia echo that ultimate enthusiasm. "Experience the true essence of nature and preserve its majestic beauty for those who follow," they advise.

In David Abram's *The Spell of the Sensuous*, he writes of humans as being in "a delicate reciprocity" with "an animate earth." We congratulate responsible Valley landowners who understand that they and their land, including all that grows and dwells there, are inseparable. By cherishing their land, and patiently caring for it, they give powerful testimony to the goodness of the whole earth.

THE WINNING
PHOTOGRAPHS

BIRDS

The time of the singing of birds is come,
and the voice of the turtledove is heard
in our land.

—The Song of Solomon

Birds of the Valley

The Rio Grande Valley has been blessed with a richness of wildlife across the spectrum, and nowhere is this more true than with birds. In a world obsessed with birds and birding, the Valley is internationally famous. We have over thirty species of birds that occur nowhere else in the nation. In addition to these specialties, our large numbers of resident birds and seasonal migrants give the Valley a bird list larger than that of most entire states. There are slightly over 900 recognized bird species that occur in the United States, and over 400 of them have been documented in the Valley. These numbers easily put the Valley on every birder's "must go" list.

This avian bonanza is no accident. Our diversity of habitat types includes beaches, bays, tidal flats, wetlands, coastal prairies, palm jungle, riparian forest, savannas, and thorn scrub. Ours is a transition zone where east meets west, where semitropical meets semi-arid and where flyways converge. The coastline is a natural funnel for migrating birds and many species find either the northernmost or southernmost extreme of their range in the Valley. Mexican species, or "accidentals," show up with enough regularity to make birding the border even more exciting. On any given day, a first U.S. record is possible. Very few areas of North America can compete with the Valley when it comes to birds.

The photographs from The Valley Land Fund contest are just a teaser of what exists here. By all means, grab your binoculars or camera and see for yourself. You don't have to go to remote spots or gain access to special places. The birds are wherever the habitat is, including your yard. In addition to all of the great private lands featured in this contest, we have a wealth of public lands available to you. Laguna Atascosa National Wildlife Refuge, Sabal Palm Grove, Santa Ana National Wildlife Refuge, Padre Island, Boca Chica, Bentsen-Rio Grande State Park, Falcon Dam, and the endless smaller tracts across the Valley provide great birding opportunities all year long.

◄ Ferruginous Pygmy-Owl

Out of twelve known species of pygmy-owls in the world, this is one of two that occur in the U.S. It ranges through most of South America, Central America, and Mexico, but only reaches into the United States in extreme South Texas and extreme southern Arizona. A cavity nester, this is one of the Valley's specialties that birders come to pursue. Recent research suggests that these little owls may be more numerous in South Texas than previously thought.

First Place
Photo: *Irene Sacilotto – Joppa, Maryland*
Land: *H. Yturria Land & Cattle Co.*

► Cooper's Hawk

This hawk, a year-round resident, is an accipiter, or woodland hawk, with short, rounded wings and a long tail that give it great agility. The Cooper's hawk is slightly larger than its very similar cousin, the sharp-shinned hawk, and both primarily feed on other birds. Roadrunners are a favorite prey of the Cooper's hawk.

Second Place
Photo: *Steve Bentsen & Laura Moore - McAllen, Texas*
Land: *McAllen Properties - James A. McAllen*

► Turkey Vulture

One of two Valley resident vultures, the turkey vulture is larger than the black vulture and has a red, unfeathered head (whereas the black vulture's head is black).
The turkey vulture soars on thermals with the wings held in a "V," called a dihedral, and rocks from side to side, seldom flapping. This carrion eater performs a valuable service in nature. It is often mistakenly called a buzzard, which is a British name for certain large hawks.

Third Place
Photo: *Wendy Shattil & Bob Rozinski - Denver, Colorado*
Land: *Cook Ranches - Jim & Kathy Collins*

WHITE IBIS

Ibises use their unique bill to probe for unseen prey. They hunt by feel and snap the bill shut on contact. They are sociable birds, often hunting in groups. They fly with their necks extended in V-formation and frequently flap or glide in unison. During the breeding season the red bill and legs of the white ibis become brilliant red.

First Place
Photo: *Tim W. Cooper - Rio Hondo, Texas*
Land: *Douglas & Jan Hardie*

◄ TRICOLORED HERON

Formerly known as the Louisiana heron, this slender bird is solitary in its feeding, but nests in colonies with other herons and egrets. Members of the heron family stalk their prey, silently moving along waiting to spear fish with their long, pointed bills. Herons and egrets fly with their necks hunched back on their shoulders, not stretched out in front of them. In addition to fish, they also eat snakes, frogs, crayfish, crabs, and insects.

Second Place
Photo: *Wendy Shattil & Bob Rozinski - Denver, Colorado*
Land: *Cook Ranches - Jim & Kathy Collins*

► ROSEATE SPOONBILL

Among our most colorful birds, roseate spoonbills are gorgeous at a distance and bizarre up close. They use their large, spoon-shaped bill to sift through the muck for prey while walking slowly forward. They are brilliant pink in the breeding season and are primarily coastal. Green Island, in the Laguna Madre near the mouth of the Arroyo Colorado, is home to a large nesting colony of roseate spoonbills.

Third Place
Photo: *Tim W. Cooper - Rio Hondo, Texas*
Land: *Douglas & Jan Hardie*

WATERFOWL

ANHINGA

Nicknamed the "snakebird" for its habit of swimming with only its head and neck above the water, the anhinga is a member of the darter family. Anhingas are tropical or subtropical birds and feed mainly on rough fish of no interest to humans. They hunt while swimming underwater. Like cormorants, but unlike other waterbirds, they have feathers that become waterlogged, so they must allow them to dry between fishing sessions. They are frequently seen perched in trees above the water with wings half-spread to dry.

Second Place
Photo: *Larry R. Ditto - McAllen, Texas*
Land: *Bill Burns*

◄ BLACK-BELLIED WHISTLING-DUCK

The Valley is home to two species of whistling-ducks. Although similarly named, whistling-ducks are quite different from other ducks. They are tropical or subtropical birds, feed both during the day and night, and make wild, whistling sounds. Black-bellied whistling-ducks often rest on low snags over the water, sit on fences, or perch high in dead trees. They are primarily seed and grain eaters, with insects and other invertebrates making up less than ten percent of the diet.

First Place
Photo: *Michael H. Francis - Billings, Montana*
Land: *McAllen Properties - James A. McAllen*

BLACK-BELLIED WHISTLING-DUCK

Black-bellied whistling-ducks frequently pair for life. Unlike most other waterfowl, male whistling-ducks actively participate in incubating the eggs and caring for the young. They are mainly cavity nesters, but occasionally will nest on the ground. Females will lay eggs in each other's nests, and some such "dump" nests may have over 50 eggs!

Third Place
Photo: *Irene Sacilotto - Joppa, Maryland*
Land: *H. Yturria Land & Cattle Co.*

► Black-necked Stilt

A very long-legged, delicate bird, the black-necked stilt lives in grassy marshes, pools, and shallow lakes. They are often seen with American avocets, but the stilt is more partial to fresh water. Insects and crustaceans such as beetles, flies, shrimp, crayfish, tadpoles, and snails form their diet. They are year-round residents of the Valley.

First Place
Photo: *Tom Tietz - Littleton, Colorado*
Land: *Guerra Brothers Ranches - A.R. Guerra*

American Avocet

The avocet can be recognized by its long, graceful, upturned bill. They feed in shallow water while leaning forward, with the tips of their bills slightly open, filtering small food items from just below the surface. Sometimes a flock will feed in unison, swinging their heads from side to side together. They are equally at home in fresh or salt water.

Second Place
Photo: *Gary Kramer - Willows, California*
Land: *Barry & Elizabeth Roberts*

Yellowlegs species

The Valley has two species of yellowlegs, the greater and the lesser. Unless some size comparison is in the picture or the subtle field marks are visible, they can be very difficult to tell apart. Birders use their size, subtle bill shape, color differences, and voices to tell them apart. They also have some personality differences. The lesser yellowlegs is often at smaller ponds, often in larger flocks, and is frequently tamer than the greater yellowlegs.

Third Place
Photo: *Larry R. Ditto - McAllen, Texas*
Land: *Bill Burns*

◀ GREEN PARAKEET

The Valley is home to two parrot-type birds—one parrot and one parakeet. Green parakeets are bright green with long, pointed tails. They are native to Tamaulipas and their existence in the Valley is controversial, some people feeling they are escaped captive birds while others thinking they come from a natural extension of range from Mexico. Regardless, they are now part of our local, resident bird population, and their numbers are growing.

First Place
Photo: *John Snyder - Corpus Christi, Texas*
Land: *Holiday Inn Fort Brown*

▲ GREEN PARAKEET

Green parakeets have found the Valley's dead palm trees very acceptable for nesting. Typically, parakeets take over woodpecker nests and enlarge the opening. Large, noisy flocks of parakeets can be seen early and late in the day in many Valley towns.

Second Place   Photo: *Brad Doherty - Brownsville, Texas*   Land: *Steve Walker*

◀ RED-CROWNED PARROT

The red-crowned parrot is the Valley's other psittacine, or parrot-type bird. They are stockier than the parakeet and have squared tails, as opposed to the parakeet's pointed tail. They also nest in cavities in dead palms that they "appropriate" from woodpeckers. They are loud, raucous birds that are frequently heard before they are seen. The red-crowned parrot is the official City Bird of Brownsville.

Third Place   Photo: *Tony Vindell - Brownsville, Texas*   Land: *Holiday Inn Fort Brown*

►Ruby-throated Hummingbird

The small ruby-throated hummingbird migrates through the Valley in the spring and fall on its long journey. Almost all ruby-throats leave North America in the fall to winter in Mexico and Central America. Some of them go from southern Canada to Costa Rica and back again each year. This incredible journey for such a small bird is made even more incredulous by the fact that some of them cross the Gulf of Mexico in a non-stop trip.

Second Place
Photo: *Charles W. Melton - Boulder, Colorado*
Land: *La Coma Ranch - Calvin Bentsen*

◄Buff-bellied Hummingbird

The buff-belly is one of our Valley specialties, and this is the only place that it can be found reliably in the United States, although it occasionally ranges up the coast to Louisiana. A fairly large hummingbird, the sexes are marked alike. Buff-bellies frequently nest in close proximity to people. They are the only hummingbird that regularly nests in South Texas.

First Place
Photo: *Charles W. Melton - Boulder, Colorado*
Land: *John & Audrey Martin*

►Buff-bellied Hummingbird

Hummingbirds are capable of flying backwards, upside down, and hovering. These little birds have an extremely high metabolic rate and must feed constantly to maintain their energy stores. They beat their wings up to 80 times per second. They eat primarily high-energy nectar and play a key role in the pollination of plants on which they feed. They also eat some insects.

Third Place
Photo: *Sandesh V. Kadur - Brownsville, Texas*
Land: *Sabal Palm Grove*

ALTAMIRA ORIOLE

Formerly known as Lichtenstein's oriole, the altamira is our most famous resident oriole. It is a Mexican species that only reaches into the United States in extreme southern Texas. Birders come from all over the world to see this bird. The sexes are marked identically and work together in nest building and rearing the young. These birds weave a large, hanging nest that blows in the breeze, thus discouraging predators and nest parasites such as cowbirds.

Second Place
Photo: *Hugh Lieck - Kingsville, Texas*
Land: *David C. Garza*

FEMALE BALTIMORE ORIOLE

Baltimore orioles weave bag-shaped hanging nests from plant fibers. Their diet consists largely of insects, especially caterpillars, including the hairy types that other birds shun. Orioles, as a group, have a sweet tooth and will readily eat fruit and berries and visit oriole or hummingbird feeders to consume sugar water.

Third Place
Photo: *John Snyder - Corpus Christi, Texas*
Land: *John & Vanessa Smith*

ORIOLES & TANAGERS

BALTIMORE ORIOLE

Baltimore and Bullock's orioles have recently been split into separate groups by taxonomists. Formerly lumped together as varieties of "northern orioles," both species pass through the Valley on their twice-yearly migration. True neo-tropicals, they spend the winter in the tropics of Latin America and the summer months nesting across the United States and Canada.

First Place
Photo: *Mike Kelly - Terrell, Texas*
Land: *Garcia Ranch - J.A. Garcia*

GREAT KISKADEE

This loud, colorful flycatcher is a Mexican species that only reaches the United States in the Valley. In addition to flycatcher behavior, they will dive into the water after fish and frogs. Permanent residents of the Valley, they are aggressive defenders of their territories and nests and are commonly seen in residential areas of Valley cities and towns.

First Place
Photo and Land: *Mike Krzywonski - Laguna Vista, Texas*

SCISSOR-TAILED FLYCATCHER

One of our most popular birds, the scissor-tail is easily recognized by its long, graceful tail. When it flies, the beautiful salmon pink under the wings becomes visible. Closely related to the kingbirds, the scissor-tail is aggressive in defending its territory and in harassing large hawks. It is a spring and summer resident of the Valley.

Second Place
Photo: *Mike Kelly - Terrell, Texas*
Land: *Garcia Ranch - J.A. Garcia*

VERMILION FLYCATCHER

Male vermilions are stunningly brilliant, while females are more muted. They feed in typical flycatcher fashion, perching on limbs or fences and flying out to capture insects. The male performs a mating flight-song, rising 50 feet in the air in a peculiar fluttering flight while singing rapidly, then swooping back to perch.

Third Place
Photo: *Lowell R. Hudsonpillar - Mission, Texas*
Land: *La Brisa Ranch - Larry & Betty Lou Sheerin*

GREEN KINGFISHER

The Valley is the only place in the nation where all three U.S. species of kingfishers can be found. The green kingfisher, smallest of the three, has been described as looking like a sparrow with the bill of a heron. It perches over water and dives to capture small fish. A permanent resident of the Valley, it nests in burrows dug in clay or dirt banks.

First Place
Photo: *Tim W. Cooper - Rio Hondo, Texas*
Land: *Douglas & Jan Hardie*

◄ Belted Kingfisher

The belted kingfisher is the most common kingfisher in North America. This pigeon-sized bird eats mainly fish, although it occasionally takes crayfish, frogs, tadpoles, aquatic insects, small mammals, young birds, and lizards. This is one of the few species of birds in which the female is more brightly colored than the male.

Second Place
Photo: *Wendy Shattil & Bob Rozinski - Denver, Colorado*
Land: *Cook Ranches - Jim & Kathy Collins*

▲ Green Kingfisher

Members of the kingfisher family have large heads, large bills, small feet, and short tails. Only six species live in all of the Americas, but there are over 80 in the Old World. They are named for their hunting technique of plunging into the water to catch fish. In the Old World, however, many species live far from water and do not feed on fish, but they still plunge to catch their prey.

Third Place
Photo: *Allen Lowe Williams - McAllen, Texas*
Land: *Rio Grande Council Boy Scouts of America*

GROOVE-BILLED ANI

These ungainly birds have large parrot-like bills, short wings, and long tails. They are common in the Valley in the summer and usually are found in groups. They primarily eat large insects, as well as spiders, lizards, fruits, and berries. They nest communally with one to four pairs sharing a common nest in which all the females lay eggs. All adults help in incubating the eggs. The group may include adult "helpers" who are not part of a breeding pair.

Second Place
Photo and Land: *Bill Burns - McAllen, Texas*

YELLOW-BILLED CUCKOO

Often called the "rain crow," the yellow-billed cuckoo inhabits Valley thickets during the summer. Unlike some European cuckoos, our North American cuckoos are not nest parasites, but build their own nests and raise their own young. Like most cuckoos, the yellow-billed cuckoo is slender and long-tailed.

Third Place
Photo: *Glenn Hayes - Markham, Texas*
Bill Draker - San Antonio, Texas
Land: *Dr. Gary M. Schwarz*

GREATER ROADRUNNER

The roadrunner is a member of the cuckoo family. They are birds of arid and semiarid terrain. Although preferring to run, they fly quite well when they must. The roadrunner can run at 15 miles per hour and faster for short bursts. It catches and eats a remarkable array of prey, including lizards, snakes, grasshoppers, beetles, tarantulas, and snails. It also will eat fruit, berries, and the eggs of other birds.

First Place
Photo: *Steve Bentsen & Laura Moore - McAllen, Texas*
Land: *McAllen Properties - James A. McAllen*

GREEN JAY

The green jay is one of two tropical jays that occur in Texas. It is strikingly different from the bluish jays of North America. The other tropical jay found in the Valley is the brown jay. In the United States, the green jay is found only in southern Texas. In this, one of the top birding hotspots in the nation, the green jay is arguably our most famous specialty. It is as loud as it is colorful, and its presence here brings large amounts of money into the Valley economy.

First Place
Photo: *Steve Bentsen & Laura Moore - McAllen, Texas*
Land: *McAllen Properties - James A. McAllen*

Great-tailed Grackle

The female great-tailed grackle is a duller brown than the glossy purplish-black males. The males have very harsh, loud voices with which they can produce a great variety of discordant calls. They are expanding their range and increasing their population within their current range.

Second Place
Photo: *Irene Sacilotto - Joppa, Maryland*
Land: *H. Yturria Land & Cattle Co.*

Great-tailed Grackle

Very controversial birds, grackles congregate in towns, parks, and parking lots at night, forming annoying roosting groups. Research has shown these birds to be very destructive to agricultural products and the nests of other birds. Reduction of grackles in controlled studies causes the populations of other birds to rise significantly. On the positive side, these birds are beautiful, have quite dramatic courtship displays, and consume large amounts of harmful grubs from agricultural fields.

Third Place
Photo: *Wendy Shattil & Bob Rozinski - Denver, Colorado*
Land: *Cook Ranches - Jim & Kathy Collins*

◀ **PAURAQUE**   Pauraques spend the daylight hours on the ground in thickets and litter. Their camouflage is so perfect that they often remain motionless and undetected by humans and predators scant inches away. Having longer legs than most nightjars, they can run with surprising speed for short distances; however, if disturbed, they will usually flutter a short distance away and immediately resume their motionless camouflaged defense. They are ground nesters, usually in open woods or near the base of trees.

Second Place   Photo: *Hugh Lieck - Kingsville, Texas*   Land: *David C. Garza*

▼ **BARN SWALLOW**   Probably our most common swallow, the barn swallow can be recognized in flight by its reddish-brown throat and its deeply forked tail. Very few people realize how beautiful the barn swallow is because they seldom see it perched. Swallows commonly build nests in buildings, under eaves, and around human habitations. Swallows, nighthawks, and bats are significant contributors to the human war on mosquitoes and they deserve our appreciation.

Third Place   Photo: *Mike Kelly - Terrell, Texas*   Land: *Garcia Ranch - J. A. Garcia*

SWALLOWS, NIGHTJARS & SWIFTS

PAURAQUE

The pauraque is our resident nightjar. Locally called a "nighthawk" or "bull bat," their hoarse, wheezing whistles can be heard at dusk and dawn throughout the Valley. They are often seen sitting in country roads at night, their reflective red eyes visible at a long distance. Pauraques, like other nightjars, feed on the wing, consuming insects.

First Place
Photo: *Michael H. Francis - Billings, Montana*
Land: *McAllen Properties - James A. McAllen*

WILD TURKEY

Benjamin Franklin preferred the wild turkey to the bald eagle as our national symbol. Although its barnyard cousin is a rather stupid creature, thus giving the slang nickname "turkey" its negative implication, the wild turkey is an extremely wary, challenging game bird.

First Place
Photo: *Irene Sacilotto - Joppa, Maryland*
Land: *H. Yturria Land & Cattle Co.*

WILD TURKEY

When the mating season is in full swing, turkey gobblers can be seen strutting around the hens, trying to look their most impressive. Fights are common, although they seldom result in injury. During this time, their plumage is a brilliant array of colors when in direct sunlight. The wattles become brilliant red when they are excited.

Second Place   Photo: *Irene Sacilotto - Joppa, Maryland*   Land: *H. Yturria Land & Cattle Co.*

WILD TURKEY

Turkeys are omnivorous, eating almost anything that is available according to the season. They are voracious consumers of acorns, leaves, seeds, grains, berries, insects, spiders, and snails. While they prefer to walk or run, they are quite graceful fliers for short distances and roost in the tops of the tallest trees. Their numbers are increasing in many areas.

Third Place   Photo: *Glenn Hayes - Markham, Texas*   Land: *Dr. Gary M. Schwarz*
                   Bill Draker - San Antonio, Texas

D O V E S

◄ COMMON GROUND-DOVE

The Valley is home to the widest variety of doves in the nation. We have seven permanent resident species and several others that "visit" on occasion. Among the permanent residents are two species of ground-doves, the common ground-dove and the Inca dove. These are the smallest of our doves, with the Inca dove being found in more urban settings and the ground-dove being found in more rural areas. Both are quite sociable and are often seen perched in pairs or small groups.

First Place
Photo: *Hugh Lieck - Kingsville, Texas*   Land: *David C. Garza*

WHITE-TIPPED DOVE

This large, ground-foraging dove was formerly called the white-fronted dove. This is another of the Mexican birds that only reach the United States in the Valley. Their low-pitched call is very similar to the sound made by blowing across the top of a bottle. It is not uncommon for white-tipped doves to nest in hanging baskets on the porches and patios of Valley homes.

Second Place
Photo: *Wendy Shattil & Bob Rozinski - Denver, Colorado*
Land: *Cook Ranches - Jim & Kathy Collins*

WHITE-WINGED DOVE

The "white-wing" is probably our most familiar dove. Due to continuing loss of suitable native habitat, these birds are becoming urban and extending their range northward. There are substantial resident populations in almost all towns and cities as far north as Dallas, although most of our local birds migrate to Mexico and Central America in the winter.

Third Place
Photo: *Glenn Hayes - Markham, Texas*   Land: *Dr. Gary M. Schwarz*
        Bill Draker - San Antonio, Texas

▶ BLACKBURNIAN WARBLER

The wood warblers, of which the Blackburnian is one, are small, bright, and active. They are constantly flitting about high in trees as they feed on insects. With over 50 species in North America, the warblers can be challenging to identify, even in their breeding plumage. When they are in their duller fall plumage, even veteran birders are sent scurrying to the field guides for help.

First Place
Photo: *Tim W. Cooper - Rio Hondo, Texas*   Land: *Douglas & Jan Hardie*

◀ ORANGE-CROWNED WARBLER

The warblers as a group are a favorite among birders, and spring migration is widely anticipated. During that time, mixed bands of warblers can be found feeding together high in the trees. Sometimes the numbers and variety of species are impressive. One of our most common local warblers, the orange-crowned is also one of the more plainly marked members of this family. Only on occasion will the orange crown be visible, usually when the bird is agitated or displaying.

Second Place
Photo: *Michael H. Francis - Billings, Montana*
Land: *McAllen Properties - James A. McAllen*

TUFTED TITMOUSE

The tufted titmouse has a plain gray crest throughout most of its range. However, in South Texas the distinctive "black-crested" variety is found. These common birds have a remarkably loud voice for such a diminutive creature. They are frequent visitors to feeders and will carry away large quantities of sunflower seeds, one at a time. The tufted titmouse is expanding its range northward, possibly with the aid of backyard feeders.

Third Place
Photo: *Glenn Hayes - Markham, Texas*   Land: *Dr. Gary M. Schwarz*
          Bill Draker - San Antonio, Texas

NORTHERN MOCKINGBIRD

Our state bird, the mockingbird is familiar to almost everyone. Its close relatives include the catbirds and thrashers, and collectively they are known as mimic thrushes. All of the members of this family have remarkable voices, and the mockingbird is no exception. It has a wide variety of songs of its own and will mimic the songs of other birds. On spring days it may sing for hours. These birds are not timid and will attack larger birds, snakes, dogs, cats, and even humans that invade their territory.

First Place
Photo: *Glenn Hayes - Markham, Texas*
        Bill Draker - San Antonio, Texas
Land: *Dr. Gary M. Schwarz*

Northern Mockingbird

Mockingbirds are largely omnivorous and exist on a wide variety of foods, depending upon what is available. Seeds, berries, insects, worms, spiders, snails, lizards, and even fish are eaten at various times. Mockingbirds are usually solitary or seen in pairs, and only infrequently are found in larger flocks.

Second Place
Photo: *David & Larry Hausman - Pilot Point, Texas*
Land: *Norma A. Canales*

Curve-billed Thrasher

Curve-billed thrashers are year-round residents of the Valley. They are secretive birds of the underbrush that get their name from their feeding habits of "thrashing" through the leaf litter in search of food. They nest in cacti, yuccas, or thorny shrubs and sometimes use the same nest more than once. Both parents actively participate in raising the young. Recent surveys suggest that this bird is declining in Texas.

Third Place
Photo: *Joseph & Lois Kertesz - Edinburg, Texas*
Land: *John & Audrey Martin*

PAINTED BUNTING

Males defend their territories by singing from raised perches, often while partially hidden in the foliage. Males will also physically fight to establish their territorial boundaries and may have more than one mate.

Second Place
Photo: *Steve Bentsen & Laura Moore - McAllen, Texas*
Land: *McAllen Properties - James A. McAllen*

PAINTED BUNTING

The multi-colored male painted bunting is so dramatically beautiful that the female is frequently overlooked. A closer look, however, will reveal the female to be strikingly beautiful as well, although in a subdued green. When seen side by side, it is hard to believe that these birds are indeed the same species. First-winter males resemble females, although by spring, telltale hints of blue on the head and red on the breast will be showing through the green plumage.

Third Place
Photo: *Steve Bentsen & Laura Moore - McAllen, Texas*
Land: *McAllen Properties - James A. McAllen*

PAINTED BUNTING

Typical of the American buntings, the male painted bunting is brightly colored and the female is quite plain. Buntings live in areas of dense low brush where they remain hidden from view most of the time. They exist on a diet of seeds and insects and are readily seen at brush country waterholes all summer. The painted bunting is easily one of the most beautiful birds in the Valley, and we are fortunate that it is our most common bunting. However, this beauty can also be a hindrance, as they are often trapped and kept as cage birds in Mexico. Their nests are also commonly parasitized by cowbirds, and studies show their numbers to be declining.

First Place
Photo: *Glenn Hayes - Markham, Texas*
　　　　 Bill Draker - San Antonio, Texas
Land: *Dr. Gary M. Schwarz*

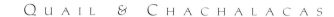
SCALED QUAIL

Locally known as the "blue quail," these birds are found in the western Valley where the drier, more hilly scrub and rock terrain is perfect habitat for them. They exist on a diet of seeds, green leaves, berries, and insects. Among hunters, the blue quail is famous for its reluctance to fly.

First Place
Photo: *Glenn Hayes - Markham, Texas*
          Bill Draker - San Antonio, Texas
Land: *Dr. Gary M. Schwarz*

NORTHERN BOBWHITE

The female bobwhite is marked similarly to the male, except the throat and eye stripe are buff, rather than white like the male. Common throughout the Valley, they love a habitat with mixed plants and grasses, which provides a variety of sources for food and cover. The bobwhite, like the scaled quail, lives and forages in coveys, except during the nesting season when they are paired.

Second Place
Photo: *Larry R. Ditto - McAllen, Texas*
Land: *San Pedro Ranch - Daniel & Baldo Vela*

NORTHERN BOBWHITE

During the mating season, the male bobwhite can be heard calling from perches as he attempts to attract an available female. Once paired, both parents work to select a site and build a nest. The nest is a depression on the ground, usually in dense growth, and lined with leaves and grass. The female will lay 12 to 16 eggs, usually one each day, but delay the start of incubation until all of the eggs are laid. The delay is to ensure that all of the young hatch within a short period of time and can leave the nest simultaneously to avoid detection by predators.

Third Place
Photo: *Larry R. Ditto - McAllen, Texas*
Land: *San Pedro Ranch - Daniel & Baldo Vela*

◀ NORTHERN CARDINAL

The cardinal shows sexual dimorphism, meaning that the sexes are marked differently. In contrast to the male's brilliant red plumage, the female is a more subdued buffy-brown. Both sexes have a reddish bill. The cardinal is a full-time Valley resident, easily attracted to seed feeders or water facilities in rural areas.

First Place
Photo: *Wendy Shattil & Bob Rozinski - Denver, Colorado*
Land: *Cook Ranches - Jim & Kathy Collins*

PYRRHULOXIA

The pyrrhuloxia is similar to the cardinal in appearance. Both have crests and are found in similar habitat. The females can easily be confused with female cardinals, but the bill of the pyrrhuloxia is yellow and is shaped differently. Also, the pyrrhuloxia is grayish in color whereas the cardinal is brownish. The males are more easily distinguished, although the male pyrrhuloxia can be quite red in breeding plumage. The pyrrhuloxia is often called the "false cardinal" or "desert cardinal."

Second Place
Photo: *Glenn Hayes - Markham, Texas*   Land: *Dr. Gary M. Schwarz*
       Bill Draker - San Antonio, Texas

NORTHERN CARDINAL

The male cardinal, or "redbird," is one of our most popular birds. Very visible and very vocal, they range as far north as Canada. They exist on a varied diet of seeds, berries, insects, spiders, caterpillars, and snails. Although the adults love sunflower seeds, the young are fed mostly insects.

Third Place
Photo: *Jeremy Woodhouse - Dallas, Texas*
Land: *Eloy Garcia*

► Eastern Meadowlark

Meadowlarks are not really larks, but rather are related to blackbirds and orioles. Common and familiar with the black "V" on their yellow chest, they are ground feeders, often seen in large groups. They are found in grasslands and open terrain where they feed on grasshoppers, crickets, beetles, caterpillars, ants, bugs, and spiders. Seeds and grains may constitute up to one-fourth of the diet.

First Place (tie)
Photo: *Tim W. Cooper - Rio Hondo, Texas*
Land: *Douglas & Jan Hardie*

Golden-fronted Woodpecker

The golden-fronted woodpecker eats a wide variety of insects, berries, nuts, fruits, and seeds. They search for insects in trees, both on the surface of the trees and by probing beneath the bark. They will crack open mesquite beans to eat the seeds. These birds will readily feed at seed feeders, suet feeders, and any source of fruit or nuts.

Second Place
Photo: *Glenn Hayes - Markham, Texas*
     Bill Draker - San Antonio, Texas
Land: *Dr. Gary M. Schwarz*

◄ GOLDEN-FRONTED WOODPECKER

The Valley has two resident woodpeckers, both of which have a striped or "ladder" back. The golden-fronted is the larger, more obvious of the two. The smaller ladder-backed woodpecker is more secretive. Like most woodpeckers, the golden-fronted has undulating flight and is quite loud and conspicuous. The male has a patch of brilliant red on top of the head which is missing in the female.

First Place (tie)
Photo: *Lance Krueger - McAllen, Texas*
Land: *El Mileño Ranch - Dr. Pedro Alonso*

EASTERN BLUEBIRD

Bluebirds are one of the most popular birds in America. Cavity nesters, they were threatened when starlings and house sparrows were introduced into North America and began competing with them for nest sites. However, many thousands of nest boxes designed to discourage their competitors and constructed along bluebird trails have saved them.

Third Place
Photo: *Mike Kelly - Terrell, Texas*
Land: *Garcia Ranch - J.A. Garcia*

MAMMALS

---

*Animals are agreeable friends—they ask
no questions, they pass no criticisms.*

—GEORGE ELIOT

Mammals of the Valley

Historically the Valley was home to a number of unique mammals that no longer are found here. Species such as jaguar, margay, and black bear have largely disappeared with the increasing development and habitat loss. However, a great variety of mammals still exists here. Some of these are quite well known and others remain hidden even to those who have spent their whole lives here.

All of South Texas is famous for its large white-tailed deer and the Valley is no exception. Hunters come from all over the nation to pursue *"el muy grande"* in our brush country. This same brush is home to other well-known mammals such as the bobcat, coyote, javelina, badger, and raccoon. However, in recent years the Valley has also become famous for harboring the last remaining U.S. populations of ocelot and jaguarundi.

In addition to these well-known and well-publicized species, our remaining native habitat has large populations of lesser known species that include bats, gophers, rats, mice, beavers, rabbits, weasels, and many others. Some of these species exist nowhere else in the United States and many of them are very specialized for life in this habitat. According to Davis & Schmidly, in their book *The Mammals of Texas*, eleven unique species of mammals that are characteristic of northeastern Mexico reach the northern limit of their range in South Texas.

One of the great enjoyments of the Valley's outdoors is the unknown. While enjoying the more common wildlife, it is always possible to encounter a coatimundi, ocelot, jaguarundi, or cougar. They still exist here marginally in spite of all we have done. As long as we protect the remaining habitat, there is hope that these now-rare species might survive.

D E E R

► WHITE-TAILED DEER

The white-tailed deer is the most important big game animal in Texas. It tends to be secretive in nature, depending on camouflage and great bursts of speed to escape predators. White-tailed deer numbers have been doing amazingly well in the past few years, showing this species' ability to adapt to human encroachment.

First Place
Photo: *Lance Krueger - McAllen, Texas*
Land: *El Mileño Ranch - Dr. Pedro Alonso*

◄ WHITE-TAILED DEER

The impressive antler racks found on white-tailed deer are only present on males. Antlers are used for sparring and dominance displays during the breeding season and follow a regular annual pattern of growth and shedding. The cycle begins with the growth of a new pair of antlers, followed by the removal of the thin skin layer that surrounds them (called velvet), and the subsequent shedding of the antlers at the end of the breeding season.

Second Place
Photo: *Glenn Hayes - Markham, Texas*   Land: *Dr. Gary M. Schwarz*
       Bill Draker - San Antonio, Texas

◄◄ WHITE-TAILED DEER

White-tailed fawns are born in the late summer after a seven-month gestation period. In keeping with their secretive nature, a mother hides her infant in the grass for a few weeks after birth until it is able to move about on its own. From that point on, the infant remains with its mother until reaching sexual maturity at two years of age. All care is provided by the female, with no assistance from the male.

Third Place
Photo: *Steve Bentsen & Laura Moore - McAllen, Texas*
Land: *McAllen Properties - James A. McAllen*

◄ Javelina

Despite appearances, peccaries, known in the Rio Grande Valley as javelinas, are not closely related to pigs. They live in groups of up to 50, with 20 being a more common number. Javelinas are highly territorial, defending their area from other herds. All individuals have rump glands, which are used to mark off the boundaries of the territory and for individual identification between herd members.

First Place
Photo: *Irene Sacilotto - Joppa, Maryland*　　　Land: *H. Yturria Land & Cattle Co.*

Javelina

Over the years, javelinas have obtained the reputation as ferocious animals. While true in some ways, this perception is somewhat skewed. While not overly aggressive, javelinas are fully able to defend themselves with their razor sharp teeth. When the situation presents itself, the herd has two general ways of dealing with predators. If a predator gets close, the entire herd scatters in different directions, creating confusion. If the predator is spotted sooner, the herd moves away, with one individual staying behind to defend the group, occasionally sacrificing its life so the remainder can escape.

Second Place
Photo: *Robert S. Simpson - McAllen, Texas*　　　Land: *Norma A. Canales*

Javelina

Females usually give birth to twins after a five-month gestation period. Births occur throughout the year. The young remain dependent on their mother for about 24 weeks. Both parents and other group members help to care for the young. In the face of danger, group members will shelter the young between their rear legs. Young are also given access to high-quality and limited food.

Third Place
Photo: *Michael H. Francis - Billings, Montana*
Land: *McAllen Properties - James A. McAllen*

▶ **MEXICAN GROUND SQUIRREL**   The Mexican ground squirrel is found throughout southern and western Texas. Unlike traditional tree squirrels, this ground-dwelling species resides in burrows that extend five feet below the surface. Occurring in the same geographic range as the spotted ground squirrel, the two species can be distinguished by the spot pattern on their back. Both species have a series of small, square-shaped spots, but only the Mexican ground squirrel's are arranged in orderly rows from head to tail.

First Place   Photo: *Charles W. Melton - Boulder, Colorado*   Land: *La Coma Ranch - Calvin Bentsen*

◀ **MEXICAN GROUND SQUIRREL**   While many burrowing species are very social, the Mexican ground squirrel tends to be more of a loner, behaving aggressively toward others that enter its territory. This tendency has resulted in each individual being responsible for its own safety. When away from their burrows, Mexican ground squirrels occasionally assume a vigilant, upright posture to scan the surrounding environment for predators and escape routes.

Second Place   Photo: *Glenn Hayes - Markham, Texas*   Land: *Dr. Gary M. Schwarz*
Bill Draker - San Antonio, Texas

▼ **MEXICAN GROUND SQUIRREL**   Hibernation is a common behavior observed in a number of ground squirrel species. Although in the Rio Grande Valley the Mexican ground squirrel is active all year long, this is not the case in more seasonal areas. In the Trans-Pecos area, they are known to have entered into hibernation no later than mid-November, with similar timing occurring in other parts of the state.

Third Place   Photo: *Charles W. Melton - Boulder, Colorado*   Land: *La Coma Ranch - Calvin Bentsen*

R O D E N T S

◄BLACK-TAILED JACKRABBIT

Despite its name, the black-tailed jackrabbit is not a true rabbit. It is a hare, a sub-group that is more adapted for speed than the traditional "rabbit." As with all rabbits and hares, the jackrabbit relies on its ability to blend in with its surroundings to escape danger. Once spotted, however, jackrabbits can flee at speeds of up to 35 miles an hour in a zigzag pattern, covering up to 20 feet in a single hop.

First Place
Photo: *Wendy Shattil & Bob Rozinski - Denver, Colorado*
Land: *Cook Ranches - Jim & Kathy Collins*

▲BLACK-TAILED JACKRABBIT   The jackrabbit's ears, as long as its hind legs, are an adaptation that aids survival. In addition to remarkable hearing, the large ears assist in the gain and loss of heat. By regulating the amount of blood that flows through the ears, the jackrabbit is able to increase or decrease its body temperature. This adaptation, along with centering its activities around dawn and dusk and its burrowing in the heat of the day, allows the jackrabbit to survive in the hot desert environment.

Second Place
Photo: *Michael H. Francis - Billings, Montana*   Land: *McAllen Properties - James A. McAllen*

◄BLACK-TAILED JACKRABBIT   All rabbits and hares are vegetarians, with dietary preferences ranging from cacti to grasses. In some areas, they have become a major competitor to livestock, with seven jackrabbits eating as much food as a single sheep. In South Texas, however, jackrabbits are largely controlled by their natural predators.

Third Place Photo: *Irene Sacilotto - Joppa, Maryland*   Land: *H. Yturria Land & Cattle Co.*

BOBCAT

Excluding the domestic cat, the bobcat is the most populous feline in North America, occurring in greater numbers than do the Rio Grande Valley's other small cats, the ocelot and jaguarundi. While actually being mid-ranged in size, the bobcat is classified as a "small cat" by its ability to purr. Scientists have divided the cats into two groups — the small cats, which purr but can't roar, and the large cats, which roar but do not purr.

First Place
Photo: *Tom Tietz - Littleton, Colorado*
Land: *Guerra Brothers Ranches - A.R. Guerra*

BOBCAT KITTENS

Bobcats have litters ranging in size from two to seven kittens, with three being the average number. These are usually born in April, following a two-month gestation period. The mother teaches the kittens to hunt and survive, this guidance continuing until fall when the young leave their mother to establish their own place in the population.

Second Place
Photo: *Mary Jo Janovsky & Michelle Moss - Harlingen, Texas*
Land: *Rio Grande Valley Shooting Center*

BOBCAT

The bobcat social system is based around the establishment of home ranges, which contain the necessary resources for daily survival — food, water, and shelter. Male home ranges tend to be larger and overlap the home ranges of several females, any of which may be courted during the breeding season. Neighboring males tend to have relatively small amounts of overlap in their home ranges, and keep track of each other through the use of scat, scrapings, and scent markings to avoid any direct confrontations.

Third Place
Photo: *Glenn Hayes -*
Markham, Texas
Bill Draker -
San Antonio, Texas
Land: *Dr. Gary M. Schwarz*

COYOTE

The coyote, whose name comes from the Aztec word *coyoti* is one of the most successful predators in North America. Since the 19th Century, the coyote has extended its range from the Great Plains to encompass the entire North American continent. This gradual expansion is due to the adaptable nature of the coyote's social system and the elimination, by man, of the coyote's main competitors, the gray wolf and the red wolf.

First Place
Photo: *Glenn Hayes - Markham, Texas*
          Bill Draker - San Antonio, Texas
Land: *Dr. Gary M. Schwarz*

COYOTE

Similar to the wolf, the coyote is known to howl in the night. While scientists still debate the exact meaning behind the calls, it is agreed that howling serves as a form of communication between pack members and between separated individuals, allowing them to find, or avoid, one another. Like humans, each coyote has a unique voice that is recognized by others, providing information not only about where they are, but who they are.

Third Place
Photo: *Gary Kramer - Willows, California*
Land: *Barry & Elizabeth Roberts*

COYOTE

The basic social unit of coyote society is the breeding pair, an adult male and female, with their offspring. Adults are monogamous and both contribute to raising the young. Although pairing is most common, coyotes are known to travel either alone or as part of a pack. In a pack, there is usually a dominant, or alpha male and female, which control the pack's movements and are the only breeding pair in the group.

Second Place
Photo: *Tom Tietz - Littleton, Colorado*
Land: *Guerra Brothers Ranches - A.R. Guerra*

NINE-BANDED ARMADILLO

Nine-banded armadillos are highly proficient burrowers. Individuals tend to have numerous dens throughout their range serving a number of purposes. Breeding dens are the deepest, up to 15 feet long and 5 feet below the surface. More common are the shallower dens used to capture food. These are checked on a regular basis for invertebrates that might have taken shelter inside.

Second Place
Photo: *Prakash Desai & Robert P. Thacker - Houston, Texas*
Land: *Perez Ranch - Betty Perez*

NINE-BANDED ARMADILLO

Always alert for possible danger, which includes, among others, hungry humans, armadillos rely on smell rather than sight. This generally nocturnal species is characterized by strong, bony armor overlaid by horn. The armor provides protection from predators, allowing the armadillo to tuck itself underneath the plates during an attack.

Third Place
Photo: *Irene Sacilotto - Joppa, Maryland*
Land: *H. Yturria Land & Cattle Co.*

► NINE-BANDED ARMADILLO

The nine-banded armadillo, also called the common long-nosed armadillo, has steadily expanded its northern geographic range to include most of Texas, Louisiana, and parts of Mississippi. However, the armadillo is very susceptible to the cold, shivering in weather we would describe as merely cool. Without proper insulation or fat storage, the armadillos have been unable to survive in areas with severe winters.

First Place
Photo: *Mike Kelly - Terrell, Texas*
Land: *Garcia Ranch - J.A. Garcia*

◄BADGER Of all the animals in the world, one would be hard pressed to find a more natural burrower than the badger. This species, found throughout all but the most eastern portions of Texas, spends the majority of its life underground or in the process of digging. Their long front claws and relatively flat shape help them to wiggle their way through tunnels at tremendous speeds.

Second Place   Photo: *Gary Kramer - Willows, California*
                    Land: *Barry & Elizabeth Roberts*

▼BADGER Although primarily nocturnal, the species of badger found in the Rio Grande Valley is known to be active at least occasionally during the day. Generally reclusive, the badger leads a solitary existence with the exception of a mother and her young. This social bond remains intact for six or seven months after the birth, at which point the family scatters.

Third Place   Photo: *Lance Krueger - McAllen, Texas*
                    Land: *El Mileño Ranch - Dr. Pedro Alonso*

MUSTELIDS - BADGERS, SKUNKS & WEASELS

◄STRIPED SKUNK

Two species of skunk, the eastern spotted skunk and the striped skunk, are found in the Rio Grande Valley. Of these, the striped skunks are the more common. Skunks are well known for their last line of defense, the spraying of a foul-smelling liquid towards an intruder up to 23 feet away. However, unlike other musk-using species, the skunk is not immune to its own scent. The raising of the tail before spraying is as much for the skunk's future well-being as to improve its aim. Interestingly, the greatest predator of the striped skunk is the great horned owl, which relies on sight and has almost no sense of smell.

First Place
Photo: *Tom Tietz - Littleton, Colorado*
Land: *Guerra Brothers Ranches - A.R. Guerra*

◀RACCOON

For a long time, raccoons were believed to prefer hollow tree cavities as den locations. Recent research has revealed that, while some females do raise their families in trees, a greater number use burrows in the ground. In these protected dens, a mother raises her offspring, between three and seven in number. She then cares for them for the first two years of life, before they strike out on their own.

Second Place
Photo: *Mike Kelly - Terrell, Texas*
Land: *Garcia Ranch - J.A. Garcia*

▶RACCOON TRACKS

Tracks in the mud are often the only indication that a raccoon has taken up residence in the area. They are primarily nocturnal and have incredible dexterous hands, which are used to gain access to areas not available to other animals. Raccoons are notorious for causing mischief and have readily adapted to coexisting with their human neighbors.

Third Place
Photo: *Michael H. Francis - Billings, Montana*
Land: *McAllen Properties - James A. McAllen*

RACCOON

Water is the main factor influencing the distribution of the common raccoon. The Latin name *lotor* means "washer," referring to the raccoon's habit of washing its food, predominantly crawfish and acorns, before eating. Even captive-reared individuals display this behavior, going through the motions of washing, whether or not water is available.

First Place
Photo: *Tom Tietz - Littleton, Colorado*
Land: *Guerra Brothers Ranches - A.R. Guerra*

GRANT'S ZEBRA

Several South Texas ranches maintain populations of exotic mammals imported from Africa and Asia. Grant's zebras are highly social animals from East Africa. They live in family groups of up to 20, sometimes forming herds of several hundred around water holes during the dry season. They are good grazers, able to survive in conditions that force antelope to move on to greener pastures. Zebras are also swift runners, an important trait since they are at the top of many predators' diets, especially those of lions.

First Place
Photo: *Michael H. Francis - Billings, Montana*
Land: *McAllen Properties - James A. McAllen*

LECHWE

The lechwe, an African antelope that ranges from the Congo to Zambia, has adapted to life in the water rather than on the land, often escaping predators by taking refuge in the shallows or even swimming. They are gregarious–forming herds of several thousand individuals. Lately, there has been an alarming decrease in the number of lechwes found in the wild, with populations being reduced to a tenth of their historical numbers.

Second Place
Photo: *Charles W. Melton - Boulder, Colorado*
Land: *La Coma Ranch - Calvin Bentsen*

FERAL PIGS

Often, the first indication of the presence of feral pigs in the area is the discovery of large holes dug into the earth. Feral pigs are descended from stock that was introduced by Europeans for sport. They are easily distinguished from their runaway ranch cousins by their heavily tufted tail and ears covered with fur. Established populations exist in the Rio Grande Valley, along the Gulf Coast, and in East Texas, where they compete with local wildlife and can have a detrimental effect on agriculture and livestock.

Third Place
Photo: *Larry R. Ditto - McAllen, Texas*
Land: *San Pedro Ranch - Daniel & Baldo Vela*

Insects & Arachnids

...the myriad things, the myriad beings, that perceptually surround us.

— David Abram

INSECTS & ARACHNIDS OF THE VALLEY

Because of the wide range of climatic conditions, from dry Chihuahuan Desert to lush subtropics, there is probably a greater diversity of insects and arachnids in the Lower Rio Grande Valley than in any other area of the United States.

Many insects and arachnids come out at night and are hard to see, hence to recognize and count. Additionally, their small size keeps us from noticing them as we might. Unlike the counting of birds or large mammals, we really don't know how many different species of insects and arachnids are buzzing, crawling, flitting, and creeping around us here in the Valley.

However, their elusive size and numbers often belie their power over us. After heavy rains, mosquitoes appear within a few days in such heavy infestations that major outdoor social events are postponed and children are kept indoors.

Cotton farmers in the Valley have become painfully aware of the might of the boll weevil in notable crash years of cotton production.

Insects beneficial to humans and often essential for the production of fruit and vegetable crops, such as ladybugs, honey bees, and wasps, may suffer from our sometimes futile efforts to control the "pests" existing alongside them.

The Valley is the only place in the United States where a specimen-rare order of the *Arachnida*, the *Palpigradi*, has ever been collected. It was found on the grounds of the old hospital in Edinburg more than fifty years ago and has never been seen there or any place else since.

Although butterfly-watching is not nearly as evident as bird-watching in the Valley, this area is a prime hunting ground for butterflies also. Numbers of butterfly species which live here are known nowhere else in the United States. This is also true of arachnids.

As for the future of insects and arachnids in the Valley, they will surely change in number and variety in response to climatic and environmental conditions, as they have for thousands of years. They deserve our respect for their incredible endurance through the ages.

TIGER SWALLOWTAIL

Common throughout North America, the tiger swallowtail is often seen on garden flowers, even in the center of cities. In the southern part of its range, as many as half of the females are brown instead of yellow. The caterpillars feed, often high up, on a variety of trees, including citrus. Tiger swallowtails are related to the colorful giant birdwing butterflies of the tropics.

First Place
Photo: *Lance Krueger - McAllen, Texas*
Land: *El Mileño Ranch - Dr. Pedro Alonso*

Monarch Butterfly

Also known as the milkweed or wanderer butterfly, the monarch butterfly is well known to the Rio Grande Valley, passing through the region on a migratory path from Canada to Mexico, where many spend the winter in communal roosts. One of the most successful species of butterfly, it can also be found in the Canary Islands, Indonesia, New Guinea, Australia, New Zealand, and other parts of the U.S.

Second Place
Photo: *Glenn Hayes - Markham, Texas*
Bill Draker - San Antonio, Texas
Land: *Dr. Gary M. Schwarz*

Common or Clouded Sulfur Butterfly

An alternate name being the mud puddle butterfly, this is one of the more common butterflies in the U.S. Its caterpillar feeds mainly on leguminous plants, and the adults may be seen in swarms feeding on damp mud, hence its alternative name. Its yellow color and markings often vary in intensity between individuals and the sexes.

Third Place
Photo: *Roland T. Scales - Burkeville, Texas*
Land: *Sharon R. Waite*

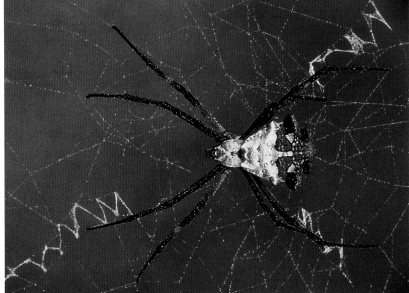

▶ FUNNEL-WEB WEAVING SPIDER

One of 14 known species of Agelenopsis in the United States, all of which look very much alike to the naked eye, the funnel-web weaving spider lives in a sheet web with a protective, funnel-like retreat at the entrance. When an insect blunders into this "front porch web," the spider explodes out on the attack. Funnel-webs may be seen in grasslands, road cuts, wooded areas, or almost anywhere that the retreat can penetrate below a rock or into a crevice or some other protected area.

First Place
Photo: *Mike Kelly - Terrell, Texas*   Land: *Garcia Ranch - J.A. Garcia*

GREEN LYNX SPIDER

Unlike most other spiders, the green lynx spider builds no web and makes its living by hunting down and physically attacking any prey that it can overcome. It has relatively good eyesight and jumps from plant to plant searching for food or a mate, as its needs dictate. It is common in cotton fields and has been known to be an effective natural control of cotton pests.

Second Place
Photo: *Mike Kelly - Terrell, Texas*   Land: *Garcia Ranch - J. A. Garcia*

SILVER ARGIOPE

From the center of its conspicuous orb web, usually in low vegetation, the silver argiope sits and waits for any insect that may fly by and become entangled in the web. In mild climates, the female deposits a walnut-sized egg sac, usually in a shrub, late in the fall and then dies. The spiderlings hatch a month or so later, but remain in the egg sac until spring, when they emerge and begin a new cycle.

Third Place
Photo: *Tim W. Cooper - Rio Hondo, Texas*   Land: *Douglas & Jan Hardie*

ROBBER FLY FEEDING ON AN ORGAN-PIPE MUD-DAUBER

Robber flies are true flies but have little in common with the flies we know best. They might be considered one of the raptors of the insect realm, attacking any prey their own size, or even larger, and subduing it mostly by strength alone. The mud-dauber is also a predator, preying mostly on spiders.

First Place
Photo: *Alex Holguin - Pleasanton, Texas*
Land: *Dr. Donald L. & Gwen Grigsby*

COMMON MUD-DAUBER

Nests of the mud-dauber can be found in barns, attics, and under bridges throughout the U.S. The wasp builds small multi-celled mounds of dried mud one cell at a time, filling the cell with spiders paralyzed by its sting and laying a single egg in the cell before sealing it. The process is repeated until the mud-dauber has a condominium for its children. Like an efficient builder, it then begins another nest.

Second Place
Photo: *Charles W. Melton - Boulder, Colorado*
Land: *La Coma Ranch - Calvin Bentsen*

HONEY BEE

Or maybe it's the Africanized bee. They are so much alike that only a bee expert can tell them apart by the way a colony reacts to a disturbance. This worker is on its way to gather nectar or pollen and has several thousand roommates that are out doing the same thing. Although we call it a "honey bee," honey production isn't as important to us as its role in pollinating fruits and vegetables.

Third Place
Photo: *Richard I. Lane, O.D. - Brady, Texas*
Land: *A.M. & Wanda Smith*

BLUE OR GREEN DAMSELFLY

The different sexes of damselflies of this family often have different colors (thus the "blue" or "green"), with the males usually more brightly colored. Sometimes, they also have different markings and change color at different stages of life. The nymphs, also called naiads, have especially hinged jaws that they use to capture prey.

Second Place

Photo: *Lance Krueger -*
McAllen, Texas
Land: *El Mileño Ranch -*
Dr. Pedro Alonso

► DAMSELFLY

All damselflies, and their distant cousins the dragonflies, are amphibious; that is, they spend part of their lives deriving oxygen from water by means of gills and another part breathing oxygen from the air through spiracles on the abdomen. They spend months as nymphs, feeding on other smaller aquatic creatures, and only three or four weeks as winged adults.

First Place

Photo: *Charles W. Melton - Boulder, Colorado*
Land: *La Coma Ranch - Calvin Bentsen*

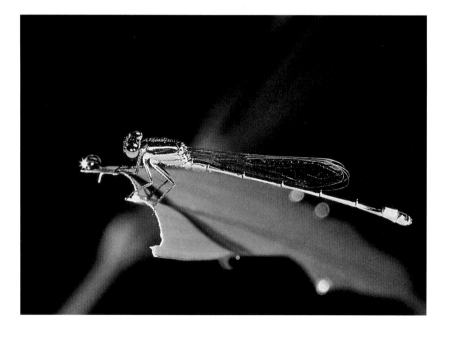

DRAGONFLY

This is a dragonfly just molted from the nymph stage to the adult stage and emerging from the water. Its typical long, narrow wings have not yet expanded to full length but will within the hour, when the dragonfly will instinctively fly away.

Third Place

Photo: *Wendy Shattil & Bob Rozinski - Denver, Colorado*
Land: *Neal & Gayle Runnels*

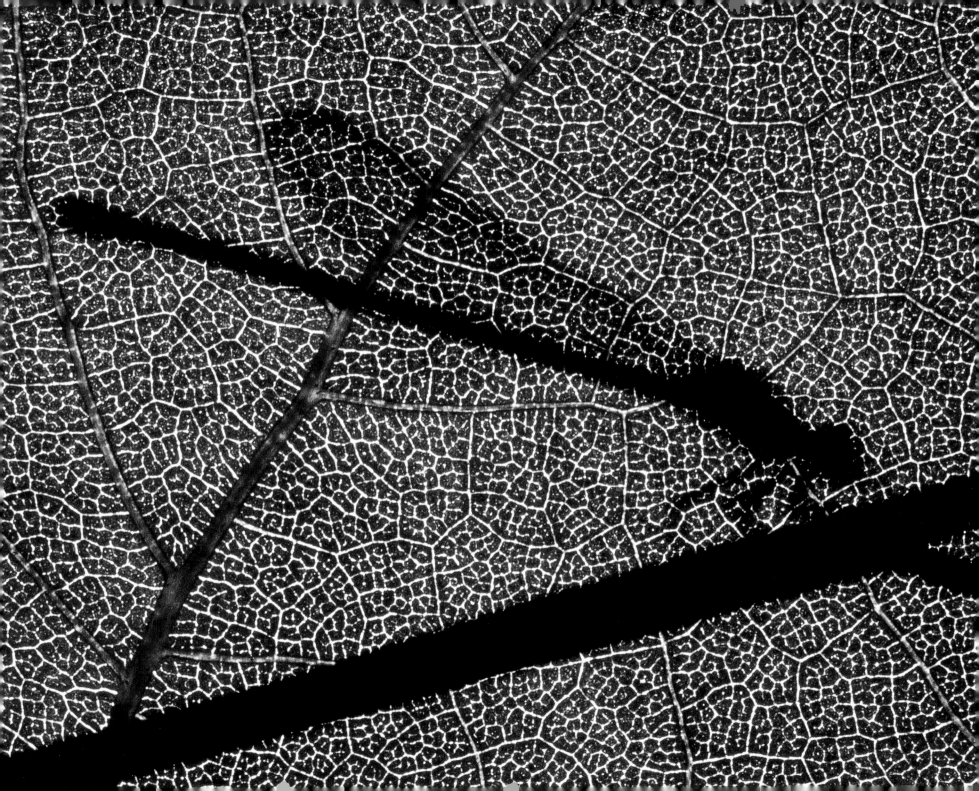

GRASSHOPPER NYMPH

One of the most easily recognized insects, the grasshopper emerges from the egg looking essentially the same as it will look when it grows up, except that it does not yet have wings. Wings will develop gradually as the insect matures. Until that time, the grasshopper must depend on its well-developed jumping legs to escape its many enemies.

Second Place
Photo: *Alex Holguin - Pleasanton, Texas*
Land: *Dr. Donald L. & Gwen Grigsby*

◀ SOLDIER BEETLE

Soldier beetles belong to the same family as the blister beetles and are relatives of the lightningbugs, or fireflies, but they neither cause blisters nor have light-producing organs. As adults, they are usually found in flowers feeding on pollen and/or nectar. Their wing covers are soft and flexible and are usually colored yellow and black.

First Place
Photo: *Charles W. Melton -*
Boulder, Colorado
Land: *La Coma Ranch -*
Calvin Bentsen

▶ KATYDID OR LONGHORNED GRASSHOPPER

This nymph will grow its wings in a few weeks and will join the summer chorus singing "katy did, katy didn't." Different species have characteristic rhythms and song patterns. The katydid, which is usually green, but may also be tan or other colors, has strong, sharp jaws and can give a person a healthy nip if handled carelessly.

Third Place
Photo: *Wendy Shattil & Bob Rozinski-*
Denver, Colorado
Land: *Cook Ranches - Jim & Kathy Collins*

Reptiles & Amphibians

A narrow fellow in the grass
Occasionally rides;
You may have met him?

—Emily Dickinson

Reptiles & Amphibians of the Valley

The Lower Rio Grande Valley comprises a very special area for the habitation of rare snakes and amphibians. Several species of snakes occur only here within the U.S. and are at the northernmost tip of their range. All of them are protected species. The Central American speckled racer occurs only in Cameron County. Among the rarest of the U.S. reptiles, it is sleek, glossy, and beautifully patterned.

Another rare Valley snake is the black striped snake. It occurs only in the United States in three of our Valley counties, Cameron, Hidalgo, and Willacy. A small, secretive snake surviving in localized suburban areas, it is mildly venomous, feeding mostly on frogs and lizards.

The Valley is the final hold-out for the northern cat-eyed snake as it is extinct in the rest of the United States. Rear-fanged and mildly venomous, it has bulging, prominent metallic-appearing eyes and elliptical pupils.

Probably the most valued snake of South Texas is the Texas indigo. It has a reputation for eating large numbers of cotton rats and killing and eating rattlesnakes. The largest snake in the state, it may reach 8 1/2 feet. It has the heaviest scales of any North American snake, designed to protect it against thorns in its native habitat, and its special skin shields it from ultraviolet radiation.

Three Valley amphibians are quite rare now and are on Texas endangered or protected lists. The black-spotted newt is native only to South Texas and northern Mexico. It resides in ponds, lagoons, and swampy areas with fairly low salinity. Always restricted somewhat in its range due to its aquatic requirements, it is even more rare now because of pesticide use, developments, and most recently, drought conditions.

The Rio Grande lesser siren is native to the lower Rio Grande and northern Mexico. Primarily carnivorous, consuming crawfish, worms, and mollusks, the lesser siren resides in warm shallow water. If the water dries up, it can burrow into the mud and secrete a mucous cocoon that dries to a protective covering. Thus it can survive a two-month dry spell.

The Mexican burrowing toad is found only in a small area in the extreme western part of the Rio Grande Valley. Its tongue is attached to the back of the mouth, a unique feature among all frogs and toads.

Herpetologists warn that these rare reptiles and amphibians of the Valley are in a very precarious position. Experts recommend care when using pesticides, keeping cats indoors whenever possible (since they hunt snakes and other small reptiles), and the avoidance of brush clearing where possible. Without refuges and the discontinuation of the clearing of their natural riparian habitats, these reptiles and amphibians have little chance for survival in the Rio Grande Valley—or anywhere.

▶ AMERICAN ALLIGATOR

This is North America's largest reptile with record lengths of over 19 feet. While normally occurring in swamps, lakes, and bayous, it can tolerate brackish water of coastal marshes such as those found in the southern tip of Texas. Although it is strong and agile in the water, it likes to spend most of its days basking in the sun.

First Place
Photo: *Wendy Shattil & Bob Rozinski - Denver, Colorado*
Land: *Cook Ranches - Jim & Kathy Collins*

AMERICAN ALLIGATOR

Digging dens deep in the mud along banks of water holes, these large reptiles hibernate during the coldest months and take refuge in them during the dry season. In early April, they emerge from hibernation with deep throaty roars to initiate the breeding season. The female deposits eggs in a large six-foot mound, where they incubate for nine weeks. High-pitched yips from the hatchlings tell the female it is time to open up the mound to let them out.

Second Place
Photo: *Mary Jo Janovsky & Michelle Moss - Harlingen, Texas*
Land: *Rio Grande Valley Shooting Center*

AMERICAN ALLIGATOR

This carnivorous animal eats just about everything, including fish, reptiles, small mammals, and waterfowl. When opportunity strikes, it will capture larger animals with its powerful jaws and twist underwater until the animal drowns. It chews underwater with the aid of a closed valve in the throat but must surface to swallow its prey.

Third Place
Photo: *Mary Jo Janovsky & Michelle Moss - Harlingen, Texas*
Land: *Rio Grande Valley Shooting Center*

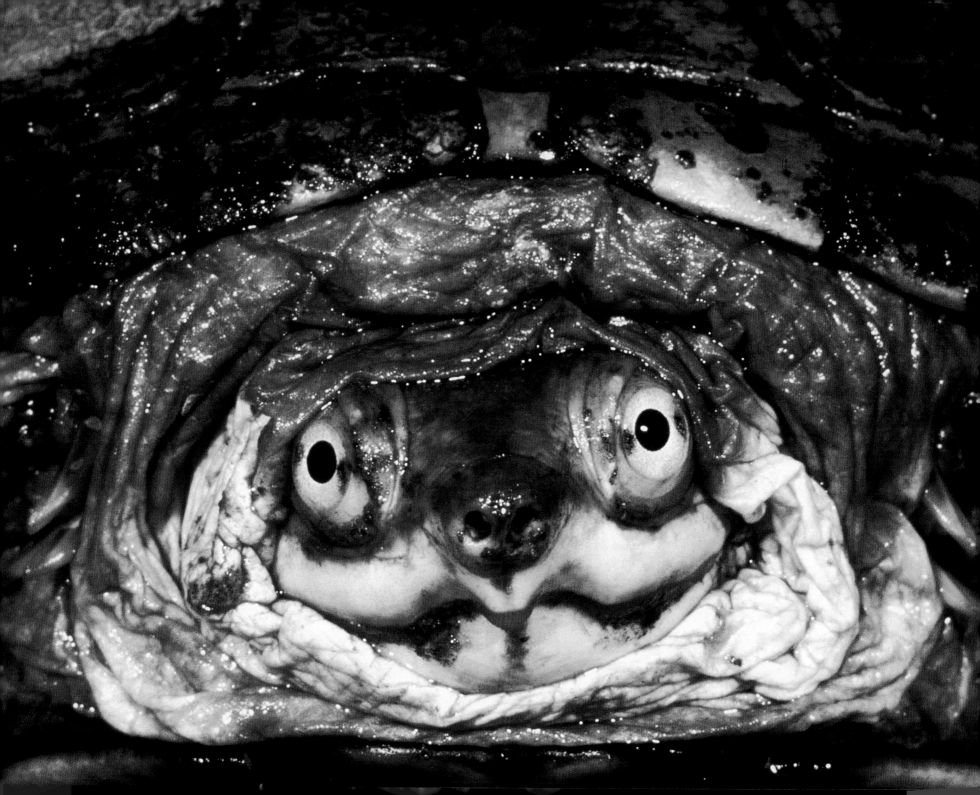

◀**YELLOW MUD TURTLE**   Primarily an aquatic bottom dweller, this olive-colored turtle is found throughout Texas except in the very eastern part. It prefers permanent bodies of water such as ponds and lakes and is even known to occur in cattle tanks. Its diet consists of invertebrates, worms, and tadpoles, which it seeks out in the muddy terrain.

First Place
Photo: *Wendy Shattil & Bob Rozinski - Denver, Colorado*
Land: *Cook Ranches - Jim & Kathy Collins*

▶**YELLOW MUD TURTLE**   This tiny turtle is smaller than an average man's hand. It reaches a length of 4 to 6 inches at maturity. When picked up or alarmed, it will secrete a foul-smelling musk from glands found on either side of its body. At six years of age or more, when these turtles reach sexual maturity, females will dig a shallow nest and deposit 1 to 6 eggs.

Second Place
Photo: *Glenn Hayes - Markham, Texas*   Land: *Dr. Gary M. Schwarz*
        Bill Draker - San Antonio, Texas

▼**TEXAS TORTOISE**   Found throughout the southern part of Texas, the Texas tortoise is most active in the early morning or late afternoon. Primarily a vegetarian, it prefers the pads, fruit, and flowers of the prickly pear cactus and can often go without water for extended periods of time, taking in moisture from this diet.

Third Place
Photo: *John English - Laredo, Texas*
Land: *Thomas E. Villarreal*

► RIO GRANDE LEOPARD FROG

These belong to a family called the true frogs. They tend to be large in size with slim waists, long legs, pointed toes, and extensively webbed feet. They are excellent jumpers and live most of their life near the water's edge where they are only a hop away from escaping predation, catching prey, or mating.

Second Place
Photo: *Jim Goin -*
Fort Worth, Texas
Land: *Neal & Gayle Runnels*

► RIO GRANDE LEOPARD FROG

A short guttural trill announces the presence of this aridity-adapted frog. It is an explosive breeder, taking advantage of the irregular Texas rains. The large dark spots overlaying its light-green-to-tan skin distinguish this from other species.

First Place
Photo: *Mike Kelly - Terrell, Texas*
Land: *Garcia Ranch - J.A. Garcia*

► GIANT TOAD

This aptly named toad, only found in the United States in the Rio Grande Valley of Texas, is seen in natural pools and arroyos, but occasionally inhabits man-made gardens and ponds. With a voracious appetite, it feeds on cockroaches, beetles, reptiles, or amphibians, avoiding predation by secreting a highly toxic substance from its skin and glands, which causes extreme discomfort and in rare cases death for animals foolish enough to bite into one.

Third Place
Photo: *Gary Kramer - Willows, California*
Land: *Barry & Elizabeth Roberts*

L I Z A R D S

◄TEXAS HORNED LIZARD

Commonly called the horny toad, it is distinguished by its
broad, flat body and prominent crown of spines on the back
of the head. It is usually observed on warm days near ant
mounds, which it exclusively feeds upon. When alarmed, it
can squirt blood from its eyes as a deterrent to predation.
Unfortunately, Texas horned lizard populations are declining,
possibly due to insecticides.

First Place
Photo: *Michael H. Francis - Billings, Montana*
Land: *McAllen Properties - James A. McAllen*

▲ MEDITERRANEAN GECKO   Introduced to Texas from the Mediterranean area,
this nocturnal reptile has adapted comfortably and is most at home on walls or ceilings of
homes and buildings near lights where their primary prey, insects, gather. Highly territorial,
when it gets into a dispute with another male, it can often be heard squeaking while defending its territory.

Second Place
Photo: *Alex Holguin - Pleasanton, Texas*   Land: *Dr. Donald L. & Gwen Grigsby*

◄ROSEBELLY LIZARD   Found mainly in South Texas, it is often confused with the
numerous related species but can be distinguished by the pink belly coloration found on the
males. Mainly terrestrial, it is often seen on fence posts and in clumps of cactus.

Third Place
Photo: *Larry R. Ditto - McAllen, Texas*   Land: *Bill Burns*

▶ BULLSNAKE

This diurnal species is heavy bodied and considered a powerful constrictor. When confronted, it will take a defensive stance, vibrate its tail and hiss loudly, by vibrating air forced through the epiglottis. One of the most widely distributed snakes in the state, this species is economically beneficial because of its voracious appetite for mice, cotton rats, and gophers.

First Place
Photo: *Bill Burns - McAllen, Texas*
Land: *Bill Burns*

▲ TEXAS INDIGO SNAKE   The largest snake in Texas, some individuals reach eight feet or more. Courtship is initiated by aggressive male foreplay including chin rubbing, neck nudging, tail twitching, and biting the female on the neck. Due to its diurnal, terrestrial habits and large size, this snake is often the inevitable target for destruction by intolerant people. As a result their numbers are dwindling.

Second Place
Photo: *Charles W. Melton-Boulder, Colorado*   Land: *La Coma Ranch-Calvin Bentsen*

▶ GULF COAST RIBBON SNAKE   Open prairie near the gulf portions of Texas is this snake's habitat. It is very active right after the summer rains, when it forages on its favorite prey, frogs and toads. If captured, ribbon snakes may discharge musk, with a very unpleasant odor, from glands at the base of the tail.

Third Place
Photo: *Hugh Lieck - Kingsville, Texas*   Land: *David C. Garza*

WESTERN DIAMONDBACK RATTLESNAKE

This large diamondback may reach a length of seven feet. It warns animals and people of its presence with a loud buzzing sound made by its rattle. When confronted, it may assume a coiled position ready to strike, but more often than not, will crawl away quickly from the intruder. Its retractable fangs, which bear venom, are essential for capturing mice and other rodents.

First Place
Photo: *Larry R. Ditto - McAllen, Texas*
Land: *Bill Burns*

WESTERN DIAMONDBACK RATTLESNAKE

Rattlesnakes are restricted to the New World. The western diamondback is commonly a trademark of Texas and is the subject of many phobias, fables, and folklore, most of which are usually unfounded. Actual death of people bitten by rattlesnakes is extremely rare. Still persecuted in the state of Texas, this beautiful animal helps keep destructive rodent populations to a minimum.

Second Place
Photo: *Glenn Hayes - Markham Texas*
        Bill Draker - San Antonio, Texas
Land: *Dr. Gary M. Schwarz*

WESTERN DIAMONDBACK RATTLESNAKE

Pit vipers, the group to which rattlesnakes belong, have deep facial pits situated between the eye and nostril on each side of the head. The pits are sensory organs used to detect and aim at heat given off by prey. Rattlesnakes have a striking distance that is just a little over half of their body length.

Third Place
Photo: *Mike Kelly - Terrell, Texas*
Land: *Garcia Ranch - J.A. Garcia*

SCENICS WITH WILDLIFE

The wonder is
how a tree scribbles on the sky
how the sky plagiarizes without shame
how the earth turns page after page of grass
and we know this to be
the only handwriting on the wall.

—JAN SEALE

SCENIC VIEWS OF THE VALLEY

In this special division known as "Scenics," the landscape co-stars with the animals. The photographer is the director, using imagination and artistic eye to stage the animals in their larger settings. The result dramatizes the magical symbiosis between animals and their environs.

Pausing to study the pictures, one realizes how terrain, vegetation, weather, and time cradle the animals.

Many pictures show water providing sustenance and quenching thirst: lagoons, resacas, settling basins, lakes, and "potholes" (natural rain-filled declivities). At times, fog and dew add an aesthetic lens.

First-time visitors to the Valley are often amazed by the flatness of the terrain. This is a geological by-product of the area's being at the mouth of a great river. The resulting rich alluvial soil and even distribution allow copious growth of vegetation such as thornbrush, yucca, prickly pear, meadow grasses, and mesquite trees, all of which protect and nourish the creatures.

This same flatness allows the Valley impressive, knowable skyscapes: a gem-blue dome, a backlight of fuchsia at sunset, a solemn eerie gold orb at sunrise. We note our own animal spirits responding with delight to such scenes and grant the possibility that the non-human beings of these pictures may be responding also, in ways forever unknowable to us.

Notice the arresting contrasts — pristine white egret against dark ancient mesquite trunk, shocking red turkey wattle near muted neutral brush. On the other hand, strain to see the camouflaged bobcat, deer, and coyote hiding in grass and brush havens. And observe how the javelina's face is comically similar in shape to the cactus on which it dines.

The unifying characteristic of these scenes is the serenity of the animals. A stillness pervades, as the creatures gaze mutely, or take a careful step along their sure pathways. What can we learn from their tranquillity? If we quiet ourselves, and take the time, we receive some of their spirit. We partake of the mysterious personae of the beasts.

In *The Spell of the Sensuous*, David Abram describes these quieting moments as those that shatter "habitual ways of seeing and feeling, leaving one open to a world all alive, awake, and aware."

So we pause, along with the animals, to consider the larger picture, the gracious abundance of our surroundings, the gifts of the land to us all.

▼ WATERFOWL

Valley waterfowl feed in early morning mist.

Second Place
Photo: *Roland T. Scales - Brownsville, Texas*
Land: *Sharon R. Waite*

► BLACK-BELLIED WHISTLING-DUCK

These ducks may perch in trees, on power lines, and on top of posts.

Third Place
Photo: *Darla Barrett - Hondo, Texas*
Land: *Billie C. Pickard*

S C E N I C S   W I T H   W A T E R F O W L

► COMMON GRACKLE & MOTTLED DUCKS

Setting and lighting show off the essence of Valley waterfowl.

First Place
Photo: *Wendy Shattil & Bob Rozinski - Denver, Colorado*
Land: *Cook Ranches - Jim & Kathy Collins*

122

► CATTLE EGRET

A huge mesquite tree serves as a vantage point for this egret, usually found quite close to cattle.

First Place
Photo: *Steve Bentsen & Laura Moore - McAllen, Texas*
Land: *McAllen Properties - James A. McAllen*

BLUE-WINGED TEAL, WHITE-FACED IBIS, AND GREATER YELLOWLEGS

"Potholes," small land indentations which only hold water part of the year, provide communities of migratory water birds needed wintertime water and nutrients.

Second Place
Photo: *Irene Sacilotto - Joppa, Maryland*
Land: *H. Yturria Land & Cattle Co.*

GREEN HERON

Perched in a conglomeration of branches, the heron shows its typical riverine habitat.

Third Place
Photo & Land: *Sharon R. Waite-Mission, Texas*

◄◄ GREAT HORNED OWL

Owls come out right at sunset and hunt several hours until they are satisfied.

First Place
Photo: *Michael H. Francis - Billings, Montana*
Land: *McAllen Properties - James A. McAllen*

◄ HARRIS' HAWK

The hawk utilizes the windmill as the highest point to perch upon in order to search for prey.

Second Place
Photo: *Richard I. Lane, O.D. - Brady, Texas*
Land: *A.M. & Wanda Smith*

► AMERICAN KESTREL

Here the kestrel oversees prospective food sources from atop a yucca, also known as a Spanish bayonet or pita.

Third Place
Photo: *Gary Kramer - Willows, California*
Land: *Barry & Elizabeth Roberts*

◄ **WILD TURKEY**

Turkeys need two basic areas, sites high above ground for roosting and open spaces for feeding.

Second Place
Photo: *Michael H. Francis - Billings, Montana*
Land: *McAllen Properties - James A. McAllen*

▶ **WILD TURKEY**

These turkeys seem to be marching toward a possible roosting site.

Third Place
Photo: *Wendy Shattil & Bob Rozinski - Denver, Colorado*
Land: *Neal & Gayle Runnels*

Wild Turkey

At one time, the Rio Grande Valley wild turkey was almost near extinction, but in recent times it has made an impressive comeback.

First Place
Photo: *Glenn Hayes - Markham, Texas*
       Bill Draker - San Antonio, Texas
Land: *Dr. Gary M. Schwarz*

►► WHITE-TAILED DEER

South Texas thorn brush provides cover, protection, and food rich in proteins and minerals for deer.

First Place
Photo: *Wendy Shattil & Bob Rozinski - Denver, Colorado*
Land: *Cook Ranches - Jim & Kathy Collins*

▼ WHITE-TAILED DEER

The doe pauses picturesquely beside a purple thistle; in an instant, she will spring into the thicket.

Second Place
Photo: *Ray Soto - Houston, Texas*
Land: *Starr Feedyards - Jack Scoggins, Jr.*

▼ WHITE-TAILED DEER

A beautiful South Texas misty sunrise suggests the buck as an enchanted creature of mythology.

Third Place
Photo: *Michael H. Francis - Billings, Montana*
Land: *McAllen Properties - James A. McAllen*

SCENICS WITH WILD CATS

◄ Bobcat

The grass serves to hide the bobcat from its prey and also from that which preys upon it.

First Place
Photo: *Michael H. Francis - Billings, Montana*
Land: *McAllen Properties - James A. McAllen*

◄ Bobcat

Too small to pose a threat to domesticated animals and not of much economic value, bobcats are allowed to thrive at will on most South Texas lands.

Second Place
Photo: *Tom Tietz - Littleton, Colorado*
Land: *Guerra Brothers Ranches - A.R. Guerra*

▲ Bobcat

This bobcat is a long way from any trees; still, it is not afraid to be out in the open meadow because it can defend itself well against all comers.

Third Place
Photo: *Mike Kelly - Terrell, Texas*
Land: *Garcia Ranch - J.A. Garcia*

Javelina

Without the prickly pear, there would be no javelina. It is their principal food and sheltering place.

Second Place
Photo: *Michael H. Francis - Billings, Montana*
Land: *McAllen Properties - James A. McAllen*

Javelina

Other animals are not eager to challenge the javelina, in part because of its razor-sharp teeth.

Third Place
Photo: *Tom Tietz - Littleton, Colorado*
Land: *Guerra Brothers Ranches - A.R. Guerra*

Scenics With Javelinas

► Javelina

Javelinas are animals uniquely associated with the Southwest. The javelina is also known as the collared peccary.

First Place
Photo: *Irene Sacilotto - Joppa, Maryland*
Land: *H. Yturria Land & Cattle Co.*

◄RACCOON

Raccoons are often found near water, looking for food or washing up after dinner.

First Place
Photo: *Tom Tietz - Littleton, Colorado*
Land: *Guerra Brothers Ranches - A.R. Guerra*

◄RACCOON

The nature photographer is lucky to get a daytime shot, since raccoons are nocturnal by nature.

Second Place
Photo: *Mike Kelley - Terrell, Texas*
Land: *Garcia Ranch - J.A. Garcia*

▲RACCOON

Raccoons are plentiful in South Texas.

Third Place
Photo: *Mike Kelly - Terrell, Texas*
Land: *Garcia Ranch - J.A. Garcia*

S C E N I C S   W I T H   R A C C O O N S

▶ COYOTE

The coyote is highly adaptable to all sorts of South Texas terrain, including shores, barrier islands, plains, brush, grasslands, and open fields.

First Place
Photo: *Tom Tietz - Littleton, Colorado*
Land: *Guerra Brothers Ranches - A.R. Guerra*

COYOTE

Although the coyote may prey on larger animals, its primary food is small mammals such as rabbits and mice.

Second Place
Photo: *Michael H. Francis - Billings, Montana*
Land: *McAllen Properties - James A. McAllen*

COYOTE

Camouflage can be used for concealment, both for hunting and for being hunted.

Third Place
Photo: *Glenn Hayes - Markham, Texas*
Bill Draker - San Antonio, Texas
Land: *Dr. Gary M. Schwarz*

SCENICS WITH REPTILES & AMPHIBIANS

TEXAS TORTOISE

The tortoise of South Texas lives in burrows, feeds on prickly pear and grasses, and can burrow into sand for protection against sudden changes in temperature.

First Place
Photo: *Michael H. Francis - Billings, Montana*
Land: *McAllen Properties - James A. McAllen*

◄ YELLOWBELLY WATER SNAKE

The snake surveys a resaca choked with plants in search of frogs, salamanders, and insects.

Second Place
Photo: *Ray Soto - Houston, Texas*
Land: *Billie C. Pickard*

▲ RED-EARED SLIDER

Sliders have two activities: sunning, such as this one is doing, and feeding in the water.

Third Place
Photo: *Charles W. Melton - Boulder, Colorado*
Land: *La Coma Ranch - Calvin Bentsen*

SCENICS WITH INSECTS & ARACHNIDS

SPIDERS

A beautiful sunrise reveals a spider web holding droplets of dew.

First Place
Photo: *Mike Kelly - Terrell, Texas*
Land: *Garcia Ranch - J.A. Garcia*

Dragonfly

The creativity of the photographer juxtaposes the smallness of the dragonfly against the greatness of a South Texas evening.

Second Place
Photo: *Charles W. Melton - Boulder, Colorado*
Land: *La Coma Ranch - Calvin Bentsen*

Butterfly

A bold sunset accentuates the silhouette of an unidentified butterfly on a grass seed head.

Third Place
Photo: *Charles W. Melton - Boulder, Colorado*
Land: *La Coma Ranch - Calvin Bentsen*

SMALL TRACT & BACKYARD

Thou unassuming commonplace of nature.

—WILLIAM WORDSWORTH

Right Outside Your Window

Stand at your back window. Look out. Chances are, you will see wildlife. It may be a dragonfly on a clothesline, a lizard on a patio stone, a flock of red-winged blackbirds on the back boundary of your plot of land. Given the tenacity of the semiarid parts of the Valley, and the fecundity of the subtropical Valley, it's hard to think of a place where the observer would not see some form of other-than-human life.

A special division of the contest was the "Small Tract and Backyard Competition." This was created for several reasons. Although greater diversity of animal life naturally exists on very large tracts of land, still there are many, many smaller areas of Valley land that are pockets of wildlife excellence. Depending on a number of factors, including location, terrain, care, and owner emphasis, small areas have their own stellar wildlife that bears highlighting.

A competition division that highlighted small tracts and backyards allowed landowners of forty acres and under—literally "the back forty"—and city dwellers the opportunity to enter the contest by means of a scaled entry fee more equitable to their holdings.

In one sense, the entire Valley Land Fund Wildlife Photo Contest is about small tracts. The criterion for any picture was focus on a specific animal or animals in an area framed by the limits of the camera's eye. And as one of our local naturalists pointed out, even the photographers entering the large-tract competition concentrated on one or more rather limited areas within the ranches, "hot spots" of diversity where wildlife gathered because of favorable conditions of food, water, and shelter.

Of course, the greatest reason to have such a grouping is what the pictures coming out of these miniature jewels tell us. They say that wildlife in the Valley is not always in the wild: it is all around us, filling the air, sipping from our birdbaths, peeking out from hedges, trundling around in our parks, perilously crossing our roads.

The pictures say that it's not necessary to own a large quantity of habitat in order to care for the exotic, the endangered, the beautiful. They send the message that paying attention to our special Valley environment, as private citizens in a democratic society and regardless of the size of our possessions, is everyone's job.

ALTAMIRA ORIOLE

Formerly called Lichtenstein's oriole, the altamira oriole is one of the top ten birds of the Rio Grande Valley for bird watchers. Nesting in Texas since the early 1950's, altamiras have undergone strong fluctuations in population levels. While increasing in the '60's and '70's, this species is now in jeopardy because of riparian habitat destruction.

Second Place
Photo: *Hugh Lieck - Kingsville, Texas*
Land: *David C. Garza*

SCISSOR-TAILED FLYCATCHER

This remarkable species is commonly seen on telephone wires near open fields. Distinguished by its long tail, the scissor-tailed flycatcher is less well known for its impressive courtship display. When courting, males descend in intricate flight patterns, terminating the descent after a series of aerial somersaults.

Third Place
Photo: *Tom Tietz - Littleton, Colorado*
Land: *John & Audrey Martin*

GREEN-BACKED HERON

The green-backed heron is most easily observed around its preferred hunting grounds, lakes, and ponds. Unlike other herons, this timid species does not like being caught out in the open, preferring to wade through the reeds and grass while hunting. Expert fishermen, green-backed herons often use feathers and insects as "fishing lures" to improve the odds of a good catch.

First Place
Photo & Land: *Joe & June Corso - McAllen, Texas*

CURVE-BILLED THRASHER

The curve-billed thrasher is a commonly occurring, year-round resident of the southwestern United States. This bird has formed a close association with a number of cactus species, finding protected nesting sites among the spines of the prickly pear.

Fourth Place
Photo: *Bill Leidner - Mission, Texas*
Land: *Alan Robert Leidner*

WHITE-WINGED DOVE

A flash of white on the wings helps to distinguish the white-winged dove from the common mourning dove. Ironically, the hunting of this species has also been its salvation. When the Texas Fish and Wildlife Department realized this game bird was suffering a population decline, a conservation program was initiated. Numbers have since increased, and the program has aided other species which use the same habitats.

Fifth Place
Photo & Land: *Joseph & Lois Kertesz - Edinburg, Texas*

Hispid Cotton Rat *(previous page)*

One of the most prolific of all mammals, a single female Hispid cotton rat is capable of raising up to nine litters, with five to ten offspring each, per year. This incredible reproductive potential can result in over 15,000 descendants from one female by the end of her first year. While population explosions do occasionally occur, predators, food availability, and disease help to keep the numbers down.

First Place
Photo: *Charles W. Melton - Boulder, Colorado*
Land: *John & Audrey Martin*

◄Desert Cottontail

As habitat varies throughout the desert cottontail's geographic range (as far north as Canada), so too does the adaptability of this species. In Texas, cottontails are found from mesquite thornforests to desert scrublands. They readily use underground burrows dug by other animals, thus earning the nickname of the "prairie-dog rabbit," and have occasionally been seen climbing trees to observe the surrounding environment.

Second Place
Photo: *Chris Gamel - Edinburg, Texas*
Land: *Neil & Lynda Haman*

►►Mexican Ground Squirrel

The Mexican ground squirrel survives mainly on green vegetation. Unbeknownst to most people, however, this species is partially carnivorous. Insects make up an important part of the diet, providing much needed protein for growth and development.

Fifth Place
Photo: *Tom Tietz - Littleton, Colorado*
Land: *John & Audrey Martin*

▼ DESERT COTTONTAIL

The desert cottontail is a commonly observed resident of the Rio Grande Valley, often found grabbing a snack on a well-groomed lawn. It is distinguished from the Valley's other rabbit, the eastern cottontail, by its slightly smaller build and proportionally longer ears.

Fourth Place
Photo & Land: *Dr. Jim Miller - McAllen, Texas*

▶ DESERT COTTONTAIL

A strict vegetarian, the desert cottontail survives on grasses, shrubs, and fallen fruits throughout most of the year. In areas with harsh winters, they are known to resort to consuming the bark off of trees to survive. Offspring are born nine months out of the year, with litters averaging three in number. The young are raised in a pear-shaped hole in the ground which the female sits over when it comes time to nurse.

Third Place
Photo: *Hugh Lieck - Kingsville, Texas*
Land: *David C. Garza*

▶ DRAGONFLY

Dragonflies' eyes are among the largest and most effective eyes in all of the insect realm. Made up of hundreds of facets, and although immovable, they command a view in all directions, up, down, forward, backward, and to the side. And because dragonflies are exceptionally agile in flight and they capture prey on the wing, such eyes serve them well. They also serve us humans well because the prey that dragonflies catch includes such pests as mosquitoes, gnats, midges, and flies.

First Place
Photo: *James Allen Murray - Arlington, Texas*
Land: *Mike & Marsha Gamel*

◀ DRAGONFLY

Whereas most dragonflies are green, yellow, or blue, these topers are usually red. They are rather slow fliers as compared to other dragonflies and are found throughout the U.S., usually around ponds.

Second Place
Photo: *Lance Krueger - McAllen, Texas*
Land: *Rita K. Roney*

TARANTULA

These are called the Texas tan by amateur arachnologists and fanciers of pet tarantulas. Females such as this one dig burrows in particular types of soil to suit their needs and seldom move far from the burrow unless disturbed. Males also live in burrows but leave them en masse at certain times of the year in search of mates. Typically all of the tarantulas found wandering around on the ground are males and nearing the end of their life.

Third Place
Photo & Land: *Luciano Guerra - Mission, Texas*

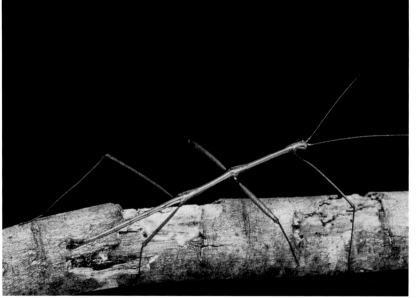

WALKING STICK

About twelve species of walking sticks are found in North America, all very similar in general view. Some tropical species are among the largest of insects, attaining a length of 9 to 13 inches. All are slow-moving, principally arboreal vegetarians. Only occasionally are they found in large numbers, but since oak foliage is a preferred diet, they sometimes denude large areas of oak forests.

Fourth Place
Photo: *James Allen Murray - Arlington, Texas*
Land: *Mike & Marsha Gamel*

Cecropia Moth

One of the largest North American moths, it is one of the silkworm moths and has been thought to have been introduced from China, its intent being for use in silk production. Its markings are variable and it is found throughout the United States.

Fifth Place
Photo & Land: *Dr. Jim Miller - McAllen, Texas*

◄ TEXAS SPINY LIZARD

Most often found clinging to the trunk of a mesquite tree, the Texas spiny lizard is easily identified by its rough scale pattern. While well-camouflaged, spiny lizards often give away their presence by the noise they make as they move up a tree away from predators.

First Place
Photo: *Jaime Rodriguez - Mercedes, Texas*
Land: *Charles Vieh*

▲ TEXAS TORTOISE

As a threatened species, the Texas tortoise has become the focus of a number of conservation efforts throughout the state. The Texas tortoise and three other species are the only native tortoises in North America.

Second Place   Photo: *Lance Krueger - McAllen, Texas*   Land: *Rita K. Roney*

◄ GIANT TOAD

This native Texas species has recently acquired international fame due to its introduction in other parts of the world. Transplanted to help control insect populations in the tropics, the giant toad has caused major ecological problems in Australia. As an exotic species, native predators of that region have not evolved to cope with the poison secreted by the toad's parotid glands.

Third Place   Photo: *Lance Krueger - McAllen, Texas*   Land: *Rita K. Roney*

► ROUGH GREEN SNAKE

A non-venomous, arboreal species, the rough green snake is often found among the leaves of trees where it hunts its primary prey: crickets, grasshoppers, and caterpillars. Non-aggressive, green snakes rely on their camouflage to protect them from predators, even going so far as to sway with the breeze to better blend in with the foliage around them.

Fourth Place   Photo: *Guillermo Aguilar - San Benito, Texas*   Land: *Lawrence V. Lof*

◄ GREEN ANOLE

Though not a true chameleon, the green anole is able to partially shift the color of its skin between green and brown. This variation permits an adaptable form of camouflage as well as allowing individuals to communicate with one another. Common around houses with trees, the green anole earns its keep by feeding on flies and mosquitoes.

Fifth Place   Photo & Land: *Kathy Kilgore - Harlingen, Texas*

◀ **BLACK-BELLIED WHISTLING-DUCK**

The subject of conservation efforts in South Texas, the population of black-bellied whistling-ducks has steadily increased to its present level. As secondary cavity nesters, whistling-ducks depend on pre-existing tree cavities for nest sites. To satisfy this need, artificial cavities, called nest boxes, can be erected, providing suitable locations in the appropriate habitat.

Second Place
Photo: *Joe Holman-Brownsville, Texas*
Land: *Wallace G. Prukop*

BLACK-BELLIED WHISTLING-DUCK
(previous page)

When temperatures drop, birds, especially water birds, risk the danger of exposure. As protection, species like the black-bellied whistling-duck have developed waterproof feathers to keep them dry. They are also adept at pulling one leg up into the feathers as they perch. While giving the appearance of having only a single leg, this behavior is actually a method of reducing heat loss.

First Place
Photo: *Charles W. Melton - Boulder, Colorado*
Land: *John & Audrey Martin*

S M A L L   T R A C T - S C E N I C S

▶ **TRICOLORED HERON**

Not a good swimmer, the tricolored heron wades into deep water with the help of its long legs. Stirring up prey as it walks near the shoreline, this bird depends on the tremendous speed of its strike to capture its prey, which include fish, amphibians, and small crustaceans.

Third Place
Photo: *Juan Luis Bonnin - Brownsville, Texas*
Land: *Episcopal Day School*

◄ RED-WINGED BLACKBIRD

Most commonly found among the cattails surrounding ponds, the red-winged blackbird is a year-round resident of the Rio Grande Valley. This species' call is one of the first announcements of the beginning of spring as individuals build small cup nests. Highly territorial, this bird forms huge flocks in the winter, occasionally numbering over a million individuals.

Fourth Place
Photo: *Allie & John Haden - South Padre Island, Texas*
Land: *Neil & Lynda Hamon*

► CURVE-BILLED THRASHER

In contrast with its drab coloration, the curve-billed thrasher is a skilled singer. Although not a mimic like the mockingbird (a distant relative), thrashers are beautiful to hear with their elaborate combination of trills and warbles.

Fifth Place
Photo: *Tom Tietz - Littleton, Colorado*
Land: *John & Audrey Martin*

SHATTIL & ROZINSKI / COOK RANCHES

BENTSEN & MOORE / McALLEN PROPERTIES

DRAKER & HAYES / SCHWARZ

COOPER / HARDIE

HONORABLE MENTIONS

Beauty is Nature's brag, and must be shown.

—JOHN MILTON

clockwise from top left:

MELTON / BENTSEN

MELTON / BENTSEN

KRAMER / EL NEGRO RANCH

KELLY / GARCIA

SHATTIL & ROZINSKI / COOK RANCHES

BENTSEN & MOORE / McALLEN PROPERTIES

BENTSEN & MOORE / McALLEN PROPERTIES

MELTON / BENTSEN

other honorable mentions are seen throughout the book

Jointly sponsored by the College of Business Administration at
The University of Texas–Pan American, The Valley Land Fund,
Kodak, Wal-Mart, and the Gladys Porter Zoo.

FOURTH GRADE
NATURE PHOTO CONTEST

*"Teach the love of nature to your children while
you can make a lasting impression."*

—JAMES ALLEN MURRAY
Photographer, 1996 VLF
Wildlife Photo Contest

Students Snap Stunners

Fourth grade students and teachers from across the Rio Grande Valley were invited to participate in a special photography contest. The purpose of the contest was to heighten the awareness of young Valleyites to the beauty and variety of our area's natural environment. To enhance the enthusiasm for the project, teachers of these fourth graders could enter a category for teachers.

Generous sponsor support by five entities—Wal-Mart Stores, Inc., Kodak, The Valley Land Fund, Gladys Porter Zoo, and the UT Pan American College of Business Administration—allowed for wide participation and worthwhile prizes and recognition.

Children entering the contest were provided with Kodak one-time-use cameras and coupons for free development at Wal-Mart.

Our Valley youngsters love a contest! A whopping 9,000 photographs were submitted, of which 800 were chosen for recognition in their schools. The second round of judging highlighted 62 student and 21 teacher photographs. These 83 award-winning photos make up the traveling exhibition of the Fourth Grade Contest.

A final round of judging by three eminent professional Valley wildlife photographers—Steve Bentsen, Larry Ditto, and Lance Krueger—brought the top winners in each class, which are presented in this book, along with a number of other notable photographs.

We congratulate the students and teachers who participated in this contest. They showed remarkable energy, initiative, and observation skills. We challenge them to keep being alert to their environment, and to help all those around them be aware of the plants, animals, and surroundings that make our Valley home so special.

EXECUTIVE COMMITTEE
Dr. Linda McCallister, Dean, College of Business Administration / UTPA
Dr. Gilbert Cardenas, Professor / Faculty Sponsor, SIFE
John Martin, President / Valley Land Fund
Colleen C. Hook, Coordinator / Valley Land Fund
Karen Hunke, President / Gladys Porter Zoo
Glen Gabardi, District Manager / Wal-Mart
Betty Smith, Management Trainer / Wal-Mart

COMMITTEE
The University of Texas–Pan American
Sara Nasif / Tina Cazares, Contest Coordinators
Volunteers from the Students in Free Enterprise (SIFE)
Volunteers from the American Marketing Association
The Valley Land Fund / Marian Della Maggiora
Jane Kittleman
Wal-Mart / Dee Ocon, Coordinator
KGBT-TV4 / Richard Moore
Region One Education Service Center / Tina Atkins, Educational Specialist

Special thanks to the *Hidalgo County Historical Museum* for hosting the nature photo display and donating Kid Passes for contestants. Proceeds from the registration fees benefitted scholarships in the College of Business Administration at UTPA.

1ST PLACE

Seagulls at South Padre Island (Title Page)

Eduardo Arron Garza
Canterbury Elementary, Edinburg

◀ **3RD PLACE**

A Mute Swan (Facing Page)

Travis Curran Hook
Oratory Academy of St. Philip Neri, Pharr

2ND PLACE

Tiger at zoo in Brownsville (Title Page)

Lillian DeaNease Gomez
McAuliffe Elementary, McAllen

▼ **4TH PLACE**

View of the Rio Grande River from Falcon State Park

John Edward Chapa
Freddy Gonzalez, Edinburg

STUDENT GRAND PRIZE PHOTOGRAPHS

▼ **5TH PLACE**

Montezuma bald cypress tree

Daniel Mark Rentfro
Episcopal Day School, Brownsville

TEACHER GRAND PRIZE PHOTOGRAPHS

▶ 2ND PLACE
*Scene in Salineño, Texas
by the Rio Grande*

Sandra Ahlman
J.F.K., La Joya

▼ 1ST PLACE
*Fence lizard on a mesquite trunk in
Sharyland backyard*

Bill Lawrence Leidner
J. Castro Elementary, Mission

3RD PLACE
Cactus blooms in backyard in Sharyland

Bill Lawrence Leidner
J. Castro Elementary, Mission

OTHER NOTABLE PHOTOGRAPHS

Clockwise from top right:

■ *Yucca in a front yard in McAllen*
Javier Robalino
Oratory Academy of St. Philip Neri, Pharr

■ *Seals at Gladys Porter Zoo*
Adrian Alex Torres
Garza Elementary, McAllen

■ *Spanish Olive Tree*
Norma Ann Escobar
Brewster School, Edinburg

■ *Thistles on a canal in Edinburg*
Raquel Marie Gonzalez
St. Joseph Catholic School, Edinburg

■ *Santa Ana Wildlife Refuge*
Cindy Zavala
Rico Elementary, Weslaco

Clockwise from top left:

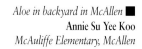

Aloe in backyard in McAllen ■
Annie Su Yee Koo
McAuliffe Elementary, McAllen

Inside Santa Ana Wildlife Refuge ■
Elsa Cantu
Victor Fields Elementary, McAllen

Green Sea Turtles at South Padre Island ■
Charlene Kroeker
Gonzalez Elementary, McAllen

Palms in San Juan ■
Jorge Perez
Z. Farias Elementary, Pharr

Clockwise from top right:

■ *Ostrich at La Coma Ranch, Red Gate, Texas*
Margaret Jo Polis
St. Joseph Catholic School, Edinburg

■ *West of my front yard near Brownsville*
Helen Denise Reed
Episcopal Day School, Brownsville

■ *Sunflower (Helianthus) and
Texas blue sky*
Jacquelyn Nicole Renaud
Valley Christian Heritage School

■ *A hackberry trunk at
Bentsen State Park*
Abigail Perez
Leal Elementary, Mission

■ *Maguey Cenizo cactus
plant in Weslaco*
Ryan Hinojosa
North Bridge, Weslaco

■ *Deer at a ranch in Willacy County*
Denise Davila
Lamar Elementary, Edinburg

Acknowledgments: Wildlife Photo Contest II

Photo Contest Judges

We were honored to have such eminently qualified judges for the Photo Contest. We extend our sincere thanks for their contributions to this event.

David Baxter
Austin, Texas
Editor, *Texas Parks & Wildlife* magazine

John Nuhn
Vienna, Virginia
Photo Editor, *National Wildlife* and *International Wildlife*, publications of the National Wildlife Federation

Thomas A. Wiewandt, Ph.D
Tucson, Arizona
Nature photographer, publisher, and owner of Wild Horizons, Inc., a photographic safari business

Sponsors

The Valley Land Fund would like to thank the business and individual sponsors for making the 1996 Wildlife Photo Contest possible. Through their commitment to the preservation of the Valley's unique natural treasures, and their vision in helping to create a new source of revenue for landowners, photographers, and businesses, they are the heart and soul of this contest and have our undying gratitude. Please visit these businesses and give them your support and heartfelt thanks. Tell them you applaud their spirit and involvement.

GRAND PRIZES

FIRST GRAND PRIZE
$15,000

Wal-Mart
"Walton Award"
A memorial to Sam and Bud Walton

SECOND GRAND PRIZE
$10,000

Boggus Motors
Texas State Bank
Valley Beverage
"Vannie Cook Award"
A memorial to Vannie Cook

THIRD GRAND PRIZE
$7,500

T. A. & Lucia Pollard
Nature Conservancy of Texas
Browning-Ferris Industries

FOURTH GRAND PRIZE
$5,000

Ann Feider & John Franks
In memory of Leone Franks

June & Carroll Elliott
In memory of Suzy Wiesendanger

FIFTH GRAND PRIZE
$2,500

Cook Game Ranches

Best of Contest

Divisions

Classes

INSECTS & ARACHNIDS

BUTTERFLIES & MOTHS	Steve & Flora Parr
ARACHNIDS	Dr. Bill & Marika Peck
BEES, WASPS & KIN	The Valley Land Fund
DRAGONFLIES & DAMSELFLIES	Schaleben Interests - Ray Schaleben
ALL OTHER INSECTS	Texas Commerce Bank

REPTILES & AMPHIBIANS

ALLIGATOR	Frank Smith Toyota - Roland Smith
TURTLES & TORTOISES	Corcoran & McClain
FROGS, TOADS & SALAMANDERS	The Valley Land Fund
LIZARDS	A.F. & Ruth Martin
NON-VENOMOUS SNAKES	Texas Commerce Bank
VENOMOUS SNAKES	Shepard, Walton & King

SCENICS WITH WILDLIFE

WATERFOWL	Palace Cleaners - Bill Stocker
WADING BIRDS	Dr. Stephen & Colleen Hook
BIRDS OF PREY	Douglas & Janet Hardie
TURKEY	Harlingen National Bank
DEER	Charles Clark Chevrolet & Clark Knapp Motors
WILD CATS	Bill & Susie Robertson in memory of John Thomas Robertson
JAVELINA	Guerra Brothers honoring Rafael & Carmen Guerra
RACCOONS	Mildred Erhart in memory of Ted Erhart
COYOTES	Color Graphics - Terry Bartelli
REPTILES & AMPHIBIANS	James A. & Frances W. McAllen
INSECTS & ARACHNIDS	The Valley Land Fund

SMALL TRACT & BACKYARD COMPETITION
40 Acres and Under

FIRST GRAND PRIZE
The Valley Land Fund

SECOND GRAND PRIZE
The Valley Land Fund

THIRD GRAND PRIZE
First Valley Bank

BEST OF CONTEST
The Valley Land Fund

DIVISIONS

BIRDS
Bill & Susie Robertson in memory of John Thomas Robertson

MAMMALS
Evelyn East in memory of Tom East Jr.

INSECTS & ARACHNIDS
The Valley Land Fund

REPTILES & AMPHIBIANS
The Valley Land Fund

SCENICS WITH WILDLIFE
Southern Texas Title

179

OFFICIAL SPONSORS

AWARDS CEREMONY   Echo Hotel & Conference Center, Edinburg
JUDGE'S ACCOMMODATIONS   Radisson Resort, South Padre Island
AIRLINE   Continental Airlines
PHOTO EQUIPMENT & PROCESSING   Britton's Photo Supply
PHOTO BLINDS   Universal Blinds

MEDIA SPONSORS

The Monitor
Brownsville Herald
Valley Morning Star
McAllen News Journal - Gregg Wendorf
KURV 710-Talk Radio - Davis Rankin
KGBT-TV 4 - Richard Moore

PHOTO EXHIBIT EVENT SPONSORS

Historic Brownsville Museum / A.G. Edwards & Sons, Brownsville

Hidalgo County Historical Museum - Edinburg
A Friend of the VLF and Museum / Edinburg Chamber of Commerce / Feldman's Valley Wide

Harlingen Chamber of Commerce
Fred Farias and Frontier Coors Distributing Company / Feldman's Valley Wide

Gladys Porter Zoo - Brownsville
The Gorgas Science Foundation / FUJI Film / Brownsville Convention & Visitors Bureau

We are also grateful to contest sponsors who display the photos in their places of business.

FOR ADDITIONAL HELP WE THANK

Raymond Jenkins - Frost Bank
Humberto Cabanas - *Rincones de mi Tierra* show on Telemundo Channel 2
Brenda Wayland Hopson - Computer Consultant
Joel Horton - Article for *Texas Co-Op Power*
Junior Service League of Edinburg
Fred Farias - Frontier Coors Distributing Company
Arturo Longoria - Article for *Texas Parks & Wildlife*
Margaret Handrow
McAllen Memorial Library
Janice Odom - Office of University Relations, UTPA
Erren Seale - Seale Design
Tina Martin - Scottie's Tours 'N Travels
Smith Fankhauser Voigt & Watson
Topp Direct Marketing

Participating Photographers

Guillermo Aguilar
San Benito, Texas

Leticia A. Alamia
Baton Rouge, Louisiana

Ruben Alaniz
Penitas, Texas

Ken Allaman
Darby, Montana

Mary Margaret Amberson
San Antonio, Texas

Charles L. Anderson
McAllen, Texas

Mike Bagby
Austin, Texas

Bart Baker
San Antonio, Texas

Julia Ruth Baker
Fort Worth, Texas

Gene Balch
Brownsville, Texas

M.C. Ball
Boerne, Texas

Korina Barraza
Brownsville, Texas

Oscar Barrera
Edinburg, Texas

Darla Barrett
Hondo, Texas

Gerry Batte
McAllen, Texas

Drew Bennie
San Benito, Texas

Jim Benson
San Benito, Texas

Steve Bentsen
McAllen, Texas

Juan Luis Bonnin
Brownsville, Texas

Steve Brewer
Fort Worth, Texas

Robert S. Brown
Weslaco, Texas

Becky Bryan
Freer, Texas

Denver Bryan
Bozeman, Montana

Bill Burns
McAllen, Texas

Fonda Marie Caffey
Abilene, Texas

J.M. Castellano
McAllen, Texas

Douglas Collins
Brownsville, Texas

Bert Condrey
Houston, Texas

Tim W. Cooper
Rio Hondo, Texas

Joe & June Corso
McAllen, Texas

Susan M. Cutney
Harlingen, Texas

Jon M. Dale
Harlingen, Texas

Lee Daughtoy
Freer, Texas

Julian W. De La Rosa
Allen, Texas

Essie Deleon
Houston, Texas

Vernon Denman
McAllen, Texas

Prakash Desai
Houston, Texas

Elisa Diaz
Edinburg, Texas

Larry R. Ditto
McAllen, Texas

Scott Ditzenberger
Carrollton, Texas

Brad Doherty
Brownsville, Texas

Bill Draker
San Antonio, Texas

Fred P. Edison
Houston, Texas

John English
Laredo, Texas

Dr. Lucile Estell
Rockdale, Texas

Dr. Don D. Farst
San Benito, Texas

Lisa J. Ferguson
Harlingen, Texas

Jorge L. Flores
Brownsville, Texas

Eddie Forshage
McAllen, Texas

Michael H. Francis
Billings, Montana

Chris Gamel
Edinburg, Texas

Don Michael Gamel
Edinburg, Texas

Irma Garcia
Santa Elena, Texas

Jesus A. Garcia
Rio Grande City, Texas

Maria L. Garcia
Linn, Texas

Pedro Garcia
Linn, Texas

Andres Garza
Sullivan City, Texas

Michael D. Garza
Mission, Texas

Gregory L. Gibson
Harlingen, Texas

Jim Goin
Fort Worth, Texas

J. Frank Gonzales
Edinburg, Texas

Garvin Granberry
Asherton, Texas

Dr. Roman R. Garza
McAllen, Texas

Hector Guerra
Edinburg, Texas

Luciano Guerra
Mission, Texas

Dennis F. Gumz
Rancho Viejo, Texas

Dr. A. H. Gutierrez, Jr.
Carlsbad, New Mexico

Allie & John Haden
South Padre Island, Texas

Jay Hardy
Madisonville, Texas

Jack Harper
San Antonio, Texas

David Hausman
Pilot Point, Texas

Glenn Hayes
Markham, Texas

Sylvia K. Henry
Dallas, Texas

Hector M. Hernandez
McAllen, Texas

Pauline M. Hernandez
McAllen, Texas

Alex Holguin
Pleasanton, Texas

Joe Holman
Brownsville, Texas

Richard Holmes
Boulder, Colorado

Lowell R. Hudsonpillar
Mission, Texas

Janet Hunter
Austin, Texas

Juan Indalecio
Edinburg, Texas

Martha Jackson
Mission, Texas

Mary Jo Janovsky
Harlingen, Texas

Grace Johnson
Harlingen, Texas

Kenneth Johnson
McAllen, Texas

Carol Jones
McAllen, Texas

Riesley R. Jones
McAllen, Texas

Sandesh V. Kadur
Brownsville, Texas

John E. Keller
Los Fresnos, Texas

Mike Kelly
Terrell, Texas

Joseph Kertesz
Edinburg, Texas

Lois Kertesz
Edinburg, Texas

Kathy Kilgore
Harlingen, Texas

Gary Kramer
Willows, California

Lance Krueger
McAllen, Texas

Mike Krzywonski
Laguna Vista, Texas

Richard I. Lane, O.D.
Brady, Texas

Bill Leidner
Mission, Texas

Hugh Lieck
Kingsville, Texas

Miguel Saenz Lopez
Rio Grande City, Texas

David H. Martinez
Mission, Texas

Raul Martinez
San Benito, Texas

Jesus Martinez, Jr.
McAllen, Texas

Ruben A. Martinez
Austin, Texas

Johnny Matthews
Keller, Texas

Mark A. Matthews
Keller, Texas

Jimmy McCorkle
Stamford, Texas

William McCorkle
Stamford, Texas

John Mealer
McAllen, Texas

Charles W. Melton
Boulder, Colorado

Dr. Jim Miller
McAllen, Texas

William Miller
Houston, Texas

Laura Moore
McAllen, Texas

Michelle Moss
Harlingen, Texas

James Allen Murray
Arlington, Texas

John P. O'Neill
Baton Rouge, Louisiana

Paul Olle
Huntsville, Texas

Ronald A. Payne
Grand Prairie, Texas

Betty Perez
Penitas, Texas

Jacob Peters
San Benito, Texas

Desiree Ponder
Brownsville, Texas

Rose Poole
Fort Worth, Texas

William E. Procter
Waco, Texas

Wallace G. Prukop
San Benito, Texas

Antonio J. Reyes
McAllen, Texas

Jaime Rodriguez
Mercedes, Texas

Reagan Ross
Rockport, Texas

Jim B. Rowland
McAllen, Texas

Bob Rozinski
Denver, Colorado

E. Ruedas
Brownsville, Texas

Irene Sacilotto
Joppa, Maryland

Vidal H. Saenz
Santa Elena, Texas

Roland T. Scales
Burkeville, Texas

John Scheiber
Brownsville, Texas

Erich Schlegel
Dallas, Texas

Wendy Shattil
Denver, Colorado

David Shekenberg
Harlingen, Texas

Robert S. Simpson
McAllen, Texas

John Snyder
Corpus Christi, Texas

Ray Soto
Houston, Texas

Jane Starling
Mission, Texas

Kern Stevenson
Bozeman, Montana

James Stewart
Edinburg, Texas

Pat Stewart
Fort McKavett, Texas

James Stuhlman
Edinburg, Texas

Robert P. Thacker
Houston, Texas

Thomas F. Thibeau
Midland, Texas

Martha Thomas
Dallas, Texas

William L. Thomas
San Antonio, Texas

Tom Tietz
Littleton, Colorado

Richard H. Topp
Harlingen, Texas

Sandra Tumberlinson
San Benito, Texas

Steve Ufkin
Harlingen, Texas

Dr. Wm. Mark Valverde
McAllen, Texas

Carlos J. Villarreal
Brownsville, Texas

Tony Vindell
Brownsville, Texas

Sharon R. Waite
Mission, Texas

Richard E. Weinland
Spring, Texas

Charles F. Weller
La Feria, Texas

Alan Wilhelm
Mission, Texas

Susan Wilhelm
Mission, Texas

Allen Lowe Williams
McAllen, Texas

Kristy Winnie
Raymondville, Texas

Josephine J. Wood
McAllen, Texas

Jeremy Woodhouse
Dallas, Texas

Sharon Wright
Mansfield, Texas

Luis M. Yzaguirre
Linn, Texas

Participating Landowners

Dr. Pedro Alonso - El Mileño Ranch
Korina Barraza
Cayetano E. Barrera, M.D.
Drew Bennie
Calvin Bentsen - La Coma Ranch
Frank N. Boggus
Jerry Brock
Robert S. Brown
Bill Burns
Mari Caballero
Norma A. Canales
Eladio Carrera
J.M. Castellano Ranch
Courtenay S. Collins
Cook Ranches - Jim & Kathy Collins
Joe & June Corso
James E. & Betty Dale
Leon Daniell
Krysti B. Davis
Larry R. Ditto
Marie & Dr. Lester Dyke
David Eanes
Evelyn East
Episcopal Day School
Dora V. Fankhauser
Dr. Don D. Farst
Mike, Luis, & Mario Flores - 3F Ranch
Mike & Marsha Gamel
Dr. Martin E. Garcia
Eloy Garcia
J.A. Garcia - Garcia Ranch
Manuel Garcia
L.A. Gardner

David C. Garza
Dr. Roman R. Garza
Maria C. Garza
Tip of Texas Girl Scouts - Camp Lulu Sams
Abel Gonzalez
B. Goodwyn
Gwen & Dr. Donald L. Grigsby
Luciano Guerra
Guerra Brothers Ranches - A.R. Guerra
Gutierrez Ranch - A.H. Gutierrez Jr., M.D.
Neil & Lynda Haman
Douglas & Jan Hardie
Carol Hill
Holiday Inn Fort Brown
Mary Jo Janovsky / Michelle Moss
Grace Johnson
Kenneth & Amy Johnson
Joseph & Lois Kertesz
Mike Krzywonski
Alan Robert Leidner
Bill Leidner
Dr. Ford & Jackie Lockett
Lawrence V. Lof
John & Audrey Martin
Bob & Margaret McAllen
McAllen Properties - James A. McAllen
John Mealer
Charlie Meyer
Dr. Jim Miller
Pete Moore
Cecilia & Robert Mumford
Nature Conservancy of Texas
Steve & Flora Parr
L.H. Pavlovich
Betty Perez - Perez Ranch
Billie C. Pickard
Desiree Ponder

Garth Prindle
Wallace G. Prukop
Al Ramirez
Rio Grande Council Boy Scouts of America
Dr. Luis M. Rios
Barry C. Roberts
Rita K. Roney
Neal & Gayle Runnels
Sabal Palm Grove
Vidal H. Saenz
Santillana Ranch - Melissa Guerra
Schaleben Interests - Ray Schaleben
Dr. Gary M. Schwarz
Larry & Betty Lou Sheerin - La Brisa Ranch
A.M. & Wanda Smith
John & Vanessa Smith
Starr Feedyards - Jack Scoggins Jr.
James Stewart
James Stuhlman
Ted & Tim Trap
Sandra Tumberlinson
Daniel & Baldo Vela - San Pedro Ranch
Robert B. Vezzetti
Charles Vieh
Carlos J. Villarreal
Thomas E. Villarreal
Sharon R. Waite
Steve Walker
Donald Vern Wernecke
Allen Lowe Williams
Bill Wilson
Josephine J. Wood
H. Yturria Land & Cattle Co.

Acknowledgemnts: Creatures on the Edge

Photo Book Committee

Editors:
Jan Epton Seale
Dr. Steve Bentsen
Colleen Curran Hook

Consultants:
Colette Hairston Adams
David Blankinship
Larry Ditto
Chris Gamel
Jane Kittleman
John & Audrey Martin
Laura Elaine Moore
Janice Odom
Father Tom Pincelli
Dr. Bill Peck
Corinna E. Rupert
Jeffery R. Rupert

Book Patron
Solicitors:
Campbell Patton
Wes Kittleman

Book Patrons

A & A Outdoors - David and Michael Adame
Herndon & Cathryn Aderhold
A. G. Edwards & Sons - Dennis Burleson
A. G. Edwards & Sons - Greg Douglas
A. G. Edwards & Sons - Georgia Mason
Alamo Bank of Texas
Dr. Pedro Alonso - El Mileño Ranch
Mr. & Mrs. Joe Charles Ballenger
Lee M. Bass - El Coyote Ranch
Steve Bentsen
Boggus Ford
Boggus Motor Co.
Boultinghouse, Simpson & Associates, Inc.
Breeden / McCumber / Gonzalez
Burton Auto Supply
Dr. Ramiro & Mari Caballero
Bob Carter & Associates
Charles Clark Chevrolet Co.
COLUMBIA Rio Grande Regional Hospital
Cook Game Ranches
Rip & Laurie Davenport
John & Marian Della Maggiora
Alice G. K. K. East
Evelyn East
Edinburg Chamber of Commerce
Ellis, Koeneke, Ramirez, LLP
Dora I. Valverde & Delmar W. Fankhauser, Jr.
First Valley Bank
Mike & Marsha Gamel
Sue Ann & J. A. Garcia, Jr.

Tony Garza, Texas Secretary of State
Betty & Lonnie Gegenheimer
Troy Giles
Barbara & Art Guerra
Guerra Brothers Successors
Gulf Coast Promotions - Julian & Rosie Garza
Harlingen Area Chamber of Commerce
Harlingen National Bank
Jack & Darlene Hart
Hidalgo County Historical Museum
Kevin D. Hiles, Inc.
Hollon Oil Company
Dr. Stephen & Colleen Hook
Dr. Phil & Laurie Howell
Dr. Phil & Karen Hunke
Inter National Bank
King Ranch, Inc.
Jarvis & Kittleman
Kreidler Funeral Home
Stephen Labuda, Jr.
The Laredo National Bank
Lee's Pharmacy - Baldo & Danny Vela
John & Audrey Martin
Mr. & Mrs. James McAllen
Robert & Margaret McAllen
McAllen Convention & Visitors Bureau
Dr. Linda McCallister
Pete & Vicki Moore
Steve & Flora Parr
Campbell A. Patton

The Payne Group
Rio Grande Valley Shooting Center
Dr. & Mrs. Luis M. Rios
Barry Coates Roberts
Bill & Susie Robertson
Jim & Donna Rowland
San Benito Bank & Trust
Schaleben Interests
Dr. Gary Schwarz
A. Clayton Scribner
Seale Design - Erren Seale
Dr. Frank E. Shepard
Dr. Stephen P. Shepard
Shepard, Walton, King Insurance Group
Stewart Title Company of Hidalgo County
Wayne & Reba Showers
Texas Commerce Bank
Texas State Bank
The University of Texas–Pan American Foundation
Thomas & Ramirez, LLP
Molly Thornberry
Valley Baptist Medical Center
Valley Beverage - Miller Lite
Valley Morning Star
Valley Nature Center
Van Burkleo & Company - Patti Van Burkleo
Sheldon & Eve Weisfeld
Willamar Gin Company
H. Yturria Land & Cattle Co.

THE VALLEY LAND FUND

is dedicated to preserving the remaining 3 to 5 percent of the natural habitat of the Lower Rio Grande Valley of Texas and the protection of the native plants and wildlife as a heritage for future generations.

Today, the VLF is working to preserve natural habitats and wildlife through the protection of land by purchase or gift and by rewarding the private landowner for responsible stewardship. In addition, the VLF is dedicated to educating people to be environmentally aware and responsible. Programs include the Wildlife Photo Contest, the Fourth Grade Nature Photo Contest, exhibitions, educational materials, and color photo books such as this one.

The Valley Land Fund
P.O. Box 2891
McAllen, Texas 78502

PHONE (956) 381-1264
FAX (956) 381-1794